A Grammar
for New Testament Greek

James M. Efird

Abingdon Press
Nashville

A GRAMMAR FOR NEW TESTAMENT GREEK

LIBRARY OF CONGRESS CATALOGING-IN-PUBLICATION DATA

EFIRD, JAMES M.
  A grammar for New Testament Greek / James M. Efird.
     p.   cm.
  Bibliography: p.
  ISBN 0-687-15678-5 (alk. paper)
  1. Greek language, Biblical—Grammar.   2. Bible. N.T.—Language, style.   I. Title.
PA817.E35   1990   89-34156
487'.4—dc20   CIP

This book is printed on acid-free paper.

Manufactured in the United States of America

For

Michelle

My Favorite Journalist

Contents

PREFACE

In the "good old days" when a person went to seminary to study biblical languages, especially Greek, the first year was spent learning the basic elements of grammar. In the second year the emphasis was on exegesis of the Greek text, learning textual criticism, and related matters. In "modern" times the emphasis is on a rapid review of the grammar in one semester, or a "cram" course in the summer, so that the student is able to get on with the business of exegesis more quickly. There are numerous reasons for this situation, but these need not be rehearsed here. Suffice it to say that most students in seminary today learn Greek in this more rapid manner.

The excellent introductory Greek grammar by J. G. Machen, *New Testament Greek for Beginners* (New York: Macmillan, 1923), is still probably the most used textbook to teach beginners the elements of Hellenistic Greek. The problem is that this book was designed for the earlier times, when a more leisurely approach was possible. Many new Greek grammars were introduced beginning in the 1960s, each having its own strengths and weaknesses, each having its own peculiar "gimmick" to allow the more rapid approach to this discipline. None has, however, really displaced Machen's work, even though it is impossible to cover that grammar in one semester and keep both students and instructor "sane."

What seems to be needed is a grammar that presents the material in the tried and tested deductive method without confusing gimmicks. The vast majority of students learn the language best in this manner, but a grammar designed for the more rapid approach was definitely needed.

Since I could not find such a grammar to use in my introductory New Testament Greek course, I began to experiment with writing one and testing it in my classes. The response was generally very positive, and through the years the students have helped to sharpen the approach and the content of this work. It is, in a sense, their product that I present here, since it has been classroom tested both in covering the material in one semester and in a concentrated summer setting.

This grammar is written for the beginning student, to introduce the basic elements of Greek grammar, vocabulary, syntactical constructions, nuances of the verbal system, etc. The emphasis is on translating from Greek into English, since this is the primary skill needed for exegesis. The exercises are designed to help the student apply the syntactical rules given in each chapter and to encourage the student to read "what is there" rather than what one thinks the sentence "should say." This is a good beginning for persons who are to come to the New Testament text itself to read what the original author really intended to say and mean. Some of the later exercises should sound familiar, since many of the sentences are taken (slightly reworked) from the New Testament itself.

This grammar is designed to be used in a classroom setting and assumes an instructor; it is not a "teach yourself" book even though a serious person could learn the elements of Greek grammar without the supporting environment of a classroom. This book is the end result of some twenty years of revising, editing, experimenting with new material, so as to make the book more useful. It is intended to be a pedagogical device to introduce the elements of Greek grammar as quickly and clearly as possible, so that involvement with the text of the New Testament itself can begin soon.

It is this involvement with the New Testament itself that makes the effort that must be exerted in learning the grammar worthwhile. It is indeed awe-inspiring to come to the sacred text to study it in the original language. It is also fun!

New Testament Greek is a form of what is known as *koinē* Greek. *Koinē* Greek represents one stage in the development of the Greek language from before 1000 B.C. to the present. The older and more formal Attic Greek was mixed with other Greek dialects and became the *koinē* Greek used by Alexander the Great. This greek became the *lingua franca* of a large segment of the world in the wake of Alexander's military victories and political agendas. *Koinē* Greek was the basic language of the era from ca. 300 B.C. until ca. A.D. 330. Differences emerged in various places as people struggled to put their thoughts into a new system of linguistic symbols. For example, there are numerous "Semitisms" in New Testament Greek because so many of the New Testament writers were formerly members of the Jewish community in Palestine. Thus, the term New Testament Greek is to be understood as the Hellenistic or *koinē* Greek of the first century A.D. tempered by the peculiarities brought to that language by the individual writers.

I cannot begin to thank all of those who have contributed positively to this project through these years. A special thanks must go, first of all, to my students, who over thirty years have really taught me more Greek than I have taught them. They have been patient, helpful, and for the most part diligent and hardworking. Second, I want to express thanks to all those graduate students who have served as teaching assistants with me since 1962. They have made valuable suggestions and have encouraged me in this project. I also want to thank the good people at Abingdon Press for their support and confidence in publishing this work, especially Dr. Davis Perkins and Ms. Ulrike Guthrie, who have been a source of encouragement and assistance in seeing this project through to completion. Deep appreciation is definitely owed to Rev. Samuel R. Smith, a recent M.T.S. graduate of the Duke Divinity School, who typed the final manuscript with care and dispatch and whose "good eye for the Greek" helped to make the final copy extremely presentable for composition. Most of all, however, I want to thank my dear wife, Vivian, who typed the manuscript in rough copy and assisted in assembling that copy in readable form for Mr. Smith. She remains a constant source of strength to me in all my endeavors.

Introduction

When the study of a foreign language is undertaken, there is always some degree of anxiety on the part of those who are preparing to study that language. Is it hard? How much time will it take? What will be the basic problem in learning this language? In the case of Greek (as with other languages) the answers are as varied as the persons who propose them.

Generally speaking, Greek is no more difficult than any other Indo-European language. It has many affinities with Latin, the Romance languages, and English. The initial shock of having to learn a new alphabet will be quickly overcome when one realizes that the Greek alphabet is very similar to the English alphabet and that the letters are quite similar in most cases.

It must be pointed out that the system of sounds presented for the letters, especially the vowels and diphthongs, is an artificial system. Scholars argue over exactly how these letters were sounded in New Testament times, but the system of sounds as presented here is generally utilized by most persons who study Greek. It is called the Erasmian system of pronunciation, after the great scholar Erasmus. Normally, therefore, one can converse with others about the Greek text and understand what words are intended no matter where one has studied.

Several helpful suggestions are presented here to assist the beginner in the task of learning New Testament Greek. First, and perhaps most important, one must review the *basic* elements of English grammar. A fundamental knowledge of English grammar will be assumed, since the Greek language has to be explained against the backdrop of another language — and that language will be English. Through the years I have found that students have had difficulty with Greek not because Greek is always complicated but because students sometimes lack a basic grasp of the terms of English grammar. What is a noun, a verb, a participle, etc.? If one does not know what these are in English grammar, it will be difficult to understand them in Greek. Therefore, if one is weak in this area or even "rusty," one would be wise to review basic English grammar before embarking on this adventure.

Second, if one does not keep up with the material *daily*, the results of getting behind can be and usually are disastrous. Setting aside some time every day, either by sitting down with the textbook or by carrying "flip cards" for vocabulary, declensions, conjugations, etc., to review in spare moments, is absolutely essential. It is still an accepted axiom that repetition is the basic law of learning, and that holds true especially for the study of language.

The verbal system is the backbone of the Greek language. Paying close attention to this system is absolutely necessary if one is to learn and understand the Greek language. It would be extremely helpful for the student to begin very early, perhaps as early as Lesson VII or VIII, to "parse" each verb form. (Parsing is the process of locating the verb form in all its individual components.) If this practice becomes a part of the student's approach early on, it will help in identifying verb forms and in learning new ones.

For example, if one finds the verb "he goes" in an English sentence, the correct parsing would be third person, singular, present, active, indicative of the verb "to go." Doing this for the Greek verbs can be of great assistance. Do not forget to parse *all* verb forms, however, not just finite verbs. Infinitives, participles, and verbs in all moods should be parsed as well. A good pattern for each is the following:

finite verb: person, number, tense, voice, mood, root
infinitive: tense, voice, root
participle: gender, number, case, tense, voice, root

Another practice that has proved helpful is for each student to prepare charts designed individually to assist in learning the verb and noun endings, specialized constructions, peculiarities of syntax and the like. No two persons learn exactly the same way; thus, the design of such charts will vary from person to person. These charts or tables will form a handy reference guide, and preparing the charts and writing down their components are further forms of repetition.

Finally, learning basic vocabulary is absolutely necessary in the study of a language. A working vocabulary of almost five hundred words will be learned during the course of using this Grammar. There is a vocabulary list provided at the back of this Grammar, but it may prove advisable for the student to begin using a good Greek-English lexicon (see bibliography) perhaps midway through the material. This will serve the purpose of acquainting one with the lexicon and also will illustrate how many different meanings and nuances some of the basic words have.

The study of Greek can be exciting. It will entail a great deal of detailed work, but the most important consideration must be that after the hard work one will be able to read the New Testament in its original language. That is the foundation stone of correct and proper exegesis and interpretation.

Lesson I

1. The Alphabet

The Greek language contains twenty-four letters. The following groupings are included as an aid for the student in learning the alphabet.

Capital Letters	Small Letters	Name	Transliteration	Sound
A	α	alpha	*a*	f*a*ther
B	β	beta	*b*	*b*at
Γ	γ	gamma	*g*	*g*o[1]
Δ	δ	delta	*d*	*d*og
E	ε	epsilon	*e*	m*e*t
Z	ζ	zeta	*z* or *dz*	*z*ag or a*dz*e
H	η	eta	*ē*	th*e*y
Θ	θ	theta	*th*	*th*in
I	ι	iota	*i*	s*i*t
K	κ	kappa	*k*	*k*eep
Λ	λ	lambda	*l*	*l*imp
M	μ	mu	*m*	*m*an
N	ν	nu	*n*	*n*ow
Ξ	ξ	xi	*x*	*ks* as lyn*x*
O	o	omicron	*o*	n*o*t or *o*mit

[1] When a gamma immediately precedes another gamma, a kappa, or a chi, it is pronounced as *n*: that is, ἄγγελος is pronounced an-ge-los.

1

Π	π	pi	*p*	po*t*
P	ρ	rho	*r*	*r*un
Σ	σ (ς)²	sigma	*s*	*s*it
T	τ	tau	*t*	*t*ow
Υ	υ	upsilon	*y* or *u*	r*u*de
Φ	φ	phi	*ph*	*ph*one
X	χ	chi	*ch*	German i*ch*
Ψ	ψ	psi	*ps*	to*ps*
Ω	ω	omega	*ō*	n*o*te

2. Vowels and Diphthongs

a. *Vowels*

There are seven vowels in the Greek language: α, ε, η, ι, o, υ, ω. Two—η and ω—are long; two—ε and o—are short by nature. α, ι, and υ may be long or short, and no outward sign will differentiate between long and short.

b. *Diphthongs*

A diphthong is two vowel sounds combined into one. There are eight in Greek—four that are combinations with ι and four that are combinations with υ:

αι = *ai*sle	αυ = h*ou*se
ει = fr*ei*ght	ευ = f*eu*d
οι = *oi*l	ηυ = f*eu*d
υι = *we*	ου = gr*ou*p

When iota combines with another vowel and that vowel is long, the iota is written under the vowel: ᾳ, ῃ, ῳ. This iota is called the *iota subscript*. In these instances the iota is not pronounced, and these are transliterated as *āi, ēi, ōi*.
All diphthongs are long except αι and οι when *final*.

ἀνθρώποις: οι long
ἄνθρωποι: οι short

---

² When sigma is the final letter of a word, it takes the form ς.

3. Classification of Consonants

This classification will be of little value at the present time. Later one will have need to refer to this table.

Labials π,β,φ
Palatals (Gutturals) κ, γ, χ
Linguals (Dentals) τ, δ, θ
Liquids λ, μ, ν, ρ
Compound consonants ζ, ξ, ψ

4. Breathing

Every Greek word that begins with a vowel or a diphthong must have a breathing mark. There are two of these marks: the *smooth breathing* (') and the *rough breathing* ('). The smooth breathing is really only a glottal stop, whereas the rough breathing is equivalent to the English *h*.

οὐ = *ou*   οὑ = *hou.*

The breathing mark is placed over the vowel before the accent mark or, in the case of a diphthong, over the second vowel of the pair, still before the accent.

Note that *initial* υ and ρ (pronounced *rh*) will receive the rough breathing.

5. Syllables

Each Greek word has as many syllables as it has vowels and/or diphthongs. When dividing a Greek word into syllables, one begins at the beginning of the word and divides one syllable from the next as soon as possible after the vowel sound. If there are two or more consonants immediately following the vowel or diphthong, the consonants generally divide, one to the syllable in question and one (or more) to the following syllable.

$$ἀδελφός = α-δελ-φος$$
$$ἄνθρωπος = αν-θρω-πος$$
$$πνεύματος = πνευ-μα-τος$$

There are three syllables which are named, and only those syllables may receive an accent: the last syllable of a word is the *ultima;* the next to the last syllable is the *penult;* the syllable before the penult is the *antepenult.*

ἄνθρωπος = αν (antepenult) θρω (penult) πος (ultima)

6. Accent

There are three marks of accentuation in Greek: the *acute* (´), the *circumflex* (˜), and the *grave* (`). To the Greek, accent probably in its origin indicated a tone or pitch, a rising or falling of the voice or both. We do not make these distinctions, and thus no differentiation of sound is made in the pronunciation of an accent; we simply stress the accented syllable, as in English pronunciation.

a. The *acute accent* may fall on any one of the last three syllables—the ultima, the penult, or the antepenult.

b. The *circumflex* may fall only on the penult or the ultima, and then only if the penult or ultima is long. If the penult or ultima is long and to be accented, that accent will be a circumflex, except where that is excluded by other rules.

δοῦλος, but δούλου

The penult may *not* receive the circumflex if the ultima is long.

c. The *grave* may stand only on the ultima. When a word originally has an acute accent on the ultima and another word follows without any intervening mark of punctuation, the acute changes to a grave.

οὐρανός, but οὐρανὸς τῆς . . .

d. The antepenult may receive only the acute accent, and it may not receive any accent if the ultima is long. Some words may be originally accented on the antepenult, but because of changes in the ultima, the accent must be moved to the penult.

ἄνθρωπος, but ἀνθρώπου

Broadly speaking, accents must be learned by applying the general rules given here with more specific rules for verbs, nouns, and other parts of speech, which will be given as these other areas of Greek grammar are presented. The best way to learn the system of accentuation is by *close observation* of the exercises. At this point there is no reason to be overly worried by accentuation rules.

7. Punctuation

The point on the line (.) in Greek is equivalent to the English period. The mark (;) indicates a question. The raised point (·) may signify English comma, semicolon, or colon. The student must determine *from the context* which is correct. (In most printed Greek texts, however, modern editors have put commas into the text. This practice means that the raised point will usually designate a semicolon or a colon.)

Exercises

A. Write the following Greek in English transliteration and divide into syllables. (Note the accents as you work.)

ἦν δέ τις ἀσθενῶν Λάζαρος ἀπὸ Βηθανίας ἐκ τῆς κώμης Μαρίας καὶ Μάρθας τῆς ἀδελφῆς αὐτῆς. ἦν δὲ Μαριὰμ ἡ ἀλείψασα τὸν κύριον μύρῳ καὶ ἐκμάξασα τοὺς πόδας αὐτοῦ ταῖς θριξὶν αὐτῆς ἧς ὁ ἀδελφὸς Λάζαρος ἠσθένει. ἀπέστειλαν

οὖν αἱ ἀδελφαὶ πρὸς αὐτὸν λέγουσαι· Κύριε, ἴδε ὃν φιλεῖς
ἀσθενεῖ. ἠγάπα δὲ ὁ Ἰησοῦς τὴν Μάρθαν καὶ τὴν ἀδελφὴν
αὐτῆς καὶ τὸν Λάζαρον.

B. Write the following in Greek characters:

*ĕn archēi ēn hŏ lŏgŏs kai hŏ lŏgŏs ēn prŏs tŏn theŏn kai theŏs
ēn hŏ lŏgŏs. houtŏs ēn ĕn archēi prŏs tŏn theŏn. panta di'
autou ĕgĕnĕtŏ kai chōris autou ĕgĕnĕtŏ oudĕ hĕn hŏ gĕgŏnĕn.
ĕn autōi zōē ēn kai hē zōē ēn tŏ phōs tōn anthrōpōn.*

Lesson II

1. Verbs

a. In order to become a competent Greek scholar, one must master the Greek verbal system. There is no substitute for hard study at this point. If the *basic* endings and peculiarities of the verb are learned well, most of the later and more complicated forms can be easily mastered. Most of the later work with the verb is simply a "variation on the theme," but the "theme" must be mastered from the beginning.

b. Each verb has the following elements:

    i. *mode* or *mood:* How the statement is made, e.g., as a fact (indicative mood) or contingently (subjunctive mood).

    ii. *voice:* The relation of the subject to the verb: i.e., does the subject act, or is the subject acted upon?

    iii. *tense:* The basic element of tense in English is time, but in Greek tense emphasizes *kind* of action more than time.

These three elements will be explained more fully as the student progresses.

c. The Greek verb is listed in the vocabulary and in Greek lexicons in the first person singular, present, active, indicative form.

2. Present Active Indicative

In the conjugation of a Greek verb there are specific

endings for *each* of the forms. The endings for the present active indicative are as follows:

	Singular	Plural
1st person	-ω	-ομεν
2nd person	-εις	-ετε
3rd person	-ει	-ουσι(ν)

Infinitive -ειν

These forms must be mastered. They will be used in other conjugations and in modified forms in other contexts.

Since the vocabulary form is first person singular, and since the ω of that form is the sign of the first person singular, the present tense stem of the verb is found by removing the ω from the vocabulary form. λύω yields λυ- as a stem. To that stem one adds the appropriate ending from the chart.

Singular		Plural	
λύω	I am loosing	λύομεν	we are loosing
λύεις	you (sg.) are loosing	λύετε	you (pl.) are loosing
λύει	he, she, or it is loosing	λύουσι(ν)	they are loosing

λύειν   to be loosing

Note. *Rule of verb accent:* The accent on the verb is *recessive*. It seeks to "go back" into the word as far as possible from the ultima. Therefore, if the ultima is long, the accent must fall on the penult. If the ultima is short, the accent must fall on the antepenult (see Lesson I 6 d).

Note that in Greek no subject necessarily need be expressed in the sentence. The subject in such cases is to be found in the verb ending.

λαμβάνουσιν   they are receiving

3. Tense

a. Tense in the Greek language generally denotes more than simple "time," i.e., present, past, or future. Tense also denotes *kind of action.* The present tense (and any other verb tense or mode built upon the present tense stem) denotes *linear* or *durative action,* action that is continuing or repetitive. This may be indicated in translation by the English "progressive" tense.

ἄγει he leads,
　　　 he is leading, *or*
　　　 he is continuing to lead

The best choice for translation to bring out the meaning of the present tense must be determined *by the context,* i.e., what the original writer intended to say in this specific setting.

b. The *active voice* indicates that the subject is doing the acting. The *indicative mode* indicates that the sentence is a simple statement; i.e., it is made as if it were a fact.

4. Movable nu

The nu (ν) after the iota of the third person plural ending is called a movable nu. Generally speaking, it is added when the final letter of the word ends in a short iota or epsilon, and when the following word begins with a vowel or diphthong or there is a mark of punctuation immediately following. By the New Testament period, however, the movable nu was used more frequently than in earlier times. *Do not add the movable nu to any form except where it is indicated* (ν) *in the paradigms of nouns or verbs.*

Vocabulary

Verbs:

ἄγω	lead, go, bring
ἀκούω	hear
βλέπω	see
γινώσκω	know
εὑρίσκω	find
ἔχω	have, hold
θέλω	wish, will
λαμβάνω	take, receive
λέγω	say, speak
λύω	loose
μέλλω	be about to
πιστεύω	believe

Conjunction:

καί	and

Exercises

A. Translate into English:

1. ἄγει, βλέπουσιν, λέγεις, πιστεύω.
2. θέλετε ἄγειν;
3. μέλλομεν εὑρίσκειν καὶ πιστεύειν.
4. ἀκούεις καὶ βλέπει καὶ λέγουσιν καὶ λαμβάνετε.
5. ἔχει καὶ γινώσκομεν.
6. θέλομεν πιστεύειν καὶ γινώσκειν;
7. μέλλω εὑρίσκειν καὶ ἔχειν.

8. θέλει βλέπειν καὶ μέλλετε ἀκούειν καὶ πιστεύειν.

B. Translate into Greek:

1. He brings; you are seeing; they are speaking; he wishes.
2. Do you wish to believe?
3. They are about to hear and to know.
4. You (pl.) are about to see and to hear and to speak.
5. Is she willing to see and to know?

Lesson III

1. Imperfect Active Indicative

a. The imperfect tense is formed on the present tense stem and thus represents action as linear or durative. To the present stem is prefixed an *augment* (ε-), which places the time in the past. The imperfect tense, therefore, represents continued action in past time. There is no one way to translate the imperfect, for the tense itself may indicate customary, repeated, prolonged, or continuing action, or even action attempted or begun. The imperfect of βαπτίζω, therefore, may be correctly translated in any one of the following ways: "I was baptizing"; "I used to baptize"; "I was continuing to baptize"; "I began to baptize"; "I tried to baptize." The correct way to translate must be determined *by the context.*

b. The imperfect tense is formed by finding the present tense stem (removing the -ω from the verb as it is found in the vocabulary), adding an augment (ε-) to the beginning of the verb and supplying the following endings:

	Singular	Plural
1st person	-ον	-ομεν
2nd person	-ες	-ετε
3rd person	-ε(ν)	-ον

Thus yielding:

ἔλυον	I was loosing	ἐλύομεν	we were loosing
ἔλυες	you were loosing	ἐλύετε	you (pl.) were loosing
ἔλυε(ν)	he, she, it was loosing	ἔλυον	they were loosing

The student must master these endings! They will be used again in other settings.

Note that the first person singular and the third person plural are identical in form. *Context* must determine which is correct if no noun or pronoun is present.

c. If the verb begins with a vowel or diphthong, changes are necessitated by the addition of the augment. The Greeks did not like vowels, especially short vowels, strung together. Therefore, the augment combined with the initial vowel or diphthong according to a particular pattern. This pattern is shown in the following tables. One notes that the two tables are identical in "outcome" but different in arrangement. Either chart produces the same result.

Augmentation Patterns

$\epsilon + \alpha \rightarrow \eta$ $\epsilon + \epsilon \rightarrow \eta$ $\epsilon + o \rightarrow \omega$

$\epsilon + \alpha\iota \rightarrow \eta$ $\epsilon + \epsilon\iota \rightarrow \eta$ (may remain $\epsilon\iota$) $\epsilon + o\iota \rightarrow \omega$ (may remain $o\iota$)

$\epsilon + \alpha\upsilon \rightarrow \eta\upsilon$ $\epsilon + \epsilon\upsilon \rightarrow \eta\upsilon$ (may remain $\epsilon\upsilon$) $\epsilon + \upsilon \rightarrow \upsilon$

$\epsilon + \iota \rightarrow \iota$ $\epsilon + \omega \rightarrow \omega$

or

$\left.\begin{array}{l}\epsilon + \alpha \\ \epsilon + \epsilon\end{array}\right> \eta$ $\left.\begin{array}{l}\epsilon + \alpha\iota \\ *\epsilon + \epsilon\iota\end{array}\right> \eta$ $\left.\begin{array}{l}\epsilon + \alpha\upsilon \\ *\epsilon + \epsilon\upsilon\end{array}\right> \eta\upsilon$ $\begin{array}{l}\epsilon + \iota \rightarrow \iota \\ \epsilon + \upsilon \rightarrow \upsilon\end{array}$

$\left.\begin{array}{l}\epsilon + o \\ \epsilon + \omega\end{array}\right> \omega$ $\epsilon + o\iota \rightarrow \omega$ (may remain $o\iota$)

*Compare the same forms above.

ἄγω, ἦγον
αἴρω, ἦρον
ἐγείρω, ἤγειρον

There are a few exceptions:

ἔχω, εἶχον
θέλω, ἤθελον
μέλλω, ἤμελλον

2. Prepositions with Verbs

In many instances in the Greek language the verb stem may be combined with a preposition. When that occurs, in forming the imperfect tense the verb stem is augmented, *not the preposition*. Further, the accent remains on the verb stem and is not placed on the preposition. (Prepositions are so distinctive in Greek that they will be readily recognizable.)

περί   around
ἄγω   go, lead
περιάγω   to go around
Imperfect: περιῆγον.

Note that neither the augment nor the accent is on the preposition.

Vocabulary

Verbs:

αἴρω	take up, bear
βαπτίζω	baptize
γράφω	write
ἐγείρω	raise up
ἐσθίω	eat

κηρύσσω	proclaim, announce
κρίνω	judge
πέμπω	send
σώζω	save
φέρω	carry, bear

Exercises

A. Translate into English:

1. ἤσθιον· ἐκήρυσσεν· εἴχομεν· ηὕρισκες· ἠκούετε.
2. ἤρετε καὶ ἐφέρετε.
3. ἤρεν καὶ ἐπίστευον καὶ ἔγραφον.
4. ἤθελες βλέπειν καὶ ἤμελλες κηρύσσειν;
5. κρίνετε καὶ ἤθελεν σώζειν καὶ βαπτίζειν.
6. μέλλομεν κηρύσσειν καὶ σώζειν;

B. Translate into Greek:

1. he had; he was judging; we were sending.
2. you are seeing; you (pl.) were continuing to baptize; we began to eat.
3. they used to send; you are about to carry; I tried to go.
4. they were about to eat; they were wishing to find.
5. Were we about to proclaim and to baptize?

LESSON IV

1. First Declension Nouns

a. There are three declensions in Greek. The first declension, or α-stem, contains primarily feminine nouns. The form of a noun given in the vocabulary is always the nominative singular, and the definite article ("the") is given with the noun.

b. There are three basic types of first declension feminine nouns. They will be designated here as the φωνή type, the καρδία type, and the δόξα type. To find the stem of the noun, the nominative singular ending is removed (-η or -α). If the noun stem ends in ε-, ι-, or ρ, the καρδία type must be followed. If the noun stem ends in a double consonant (ζ-, ξ-, or ψ-) or a double sigma (σσ-), the δόξα type must be followed. Almost all of the other nouns of the first declension follow the φωνή type. These changes occur only in the singular; the plural is not altered from one type to another.

c. There is only one set of endings for the feminine definite article. The changes in the noun endings (of the types) do not affect the article at all. The definite article acts much like an adjective with the noun; that is, it must agree with the noun in gender, number, and case.

d. There is no indefinite article ("a" or "an") in Greek. A Greek noun without an article may be translated either "a book" or "book." Usually if a noun does not have the definite article, the definite article is not to be used in the translation. (Later it will be seen that there is an anarthrous use of nouns; i.e., the noun does not have the definite

16

article but is assumed *from the context* to be definite.)

e. Frequently in Greek when a noun is more "abstract," usually in the first declension with feminine nouns, the definite article is used, but it is not translated into English. For example, one finds ἡ ἀγάπη, but this is usually translated simply as "love" rather than "the love" unless, of course, the *context* dictates otherwise.

2. Cases

In English there are three cases: nominative, possessive, and objective. Except for the apostrophe + *s* of the possessive, there is usually no change in the English word from the nominative to the objective case. (English does have such changes in its pronouns, however.) In Greek, each case is easily distinguishable by a specific ending. The cases have different functions.

nominative: This corresponds to the English nominative. The subject and predicate nominative are in the nominative case.

genitive: This is the case that usually indicates "source." It is also called the "specifying" or "whence" case. A noun in the genitive case is usually translated by the phrase "of the . . ." or "from the . . . ." No preposition is needed in Greek to express "of" or "from" (even though the student will later learn prepositions that have these meanings).

τῆς δόξης
of the glory *or*
from the glory

Context must determine which.

dative: There are three basic usages of the dative.
i. The "true" dative, the case of "personal interest." A noun in the dative case is usually

> translated with the English prepositions "to" or "for" corresponding roughly to the English indirect object.
>
> ii. The dative of place (some refer to this as the locative case), usually translated by the English prepositions "in," "at," "by." By the New Testament period this usage had been replaced for the most part by prepositions with these meanings, the most common being ἐν ("in") + the dative case.
>
> iii. The dative of instrument or means (some call this the instrumental case), is usually expressed in English by "with" or "by means of."
>
> *Context* must determine *which* of the usages is intended.

accusative: This case usually indicates extension. The direct objects of verbs are usually in the accusative case, and this case is also used with many prepositions.

vocative: This is the case of direct address, e.g., "O people, . . ."

3. Types of First Declension Nouns

a. *Endings for Nouns of the First Declension:*

φωνή type

	Singular	Plural
Nom.	-η	-αι
Gen.	-ης	-ων
Dat.	-ῃ	-αις
Acc.	-ην	-ας
Voc.	-η	-αι

καρδία type

Nom.	-α	-αι
Gen.	-ας	-ων
Dat.	-ᾳ	-αις
Acc.	-αν	-ας
Voc.	-α	-αι

δόξα type

Nom.	-α	-αι
Gen.	-ης	-ων
Dat.	-ῃ	-αις
Acc.	-αν	-ας
Voc.	-α	-αι

b. *The Feminine Definite Article*

	Singular	**Plural**
Nom.	ἡ	αἱ
Gen.	τῆς	τῶν
Dat.	τῇ	ταῖς
Acc.	τήν	τάς

c. *Full Declensions*

	Singular	**Plural**
Nom.	ἡ φωνή	αἱ φωναί
Gen.	τῆς φωνῆς	τῶν φωνῶν
Dat.	τῇ φωνῇ	ταῖς φωναῖς
Acc.	τὴν φωνήν	τὰς φωνάς
Voc.	φωνή	φωναί

Nom.	ἡ καρδία	αἱ καρδίαι
Gen.	τῆς καρδίας	τῶν καρδιῶν
Dat.	τῇ καρδίᾳ	ταῖς καρδίαις
Acc.	τὴν καρδίαν	τὰς καρδίας
Voc.	καρδία	καρδίαι

Nom.	ἡ δόξα	αἱ δόξαι	
Gen.	τῆς δόξης	τῶν δοξῶν	
Dat.	τῇ δόξῃ	ταῖς δόξαις	
Acc.	τὴν δόξαν	τὰς δόξας	
Voc.	δόξα	δόξαι	

4. Noun Accent

Several things must be noted about the declension of nouns:

    a. *General Rules for Noun Accent*

        i. There is no general rule to determine where the accent will fall on a noun. The position of the accent must be learned with the word.

        ii. The general rule for accentuation in noun declension is that *the accent* on a noun *will remain where it was in the nominative singular insofar as this is possible.*

        iii. Usually the nominative and accusative, singular and plural, do not take a circumflex accent on the ultima even if the ultima is long and to be accented.

    b. *Specific Rule for the First Declension*

In the first declension the genitive plural is accented with a circumflex on the ultima no matter where the accent was in the nominative singular; see paradigms.

5. Word Order

No set rule can be given for word order in Greek. Generally speaking, it is similar to that of English sentences. Usually the word or words to be emphasized are placed first, and the components (i.e., subject, verb, object, etc.) of the sentences can be readily recognized by the distinctive endings.

A noun in the genitive case is usually placed immediately after the noun to which it is attached. One must be careful not to rearrange genitival phrases in Greek sentences.

ἡ ἀγάπη τῆς σοφίας ἄγει εἰρήνην.
The love of wisdom brings peace.
Not (The) love brings peace of wisdom.

Vocabulary

Nouns:

ἡ ἀγάπη	love
ἡ ἁμαρτία	sin, missing the mark
ἡ ἀρχή	beginning
ἡ βασιλεία	kingdom
ἡ δόξα	glory
ἡ εἰρήνη	peace
ἡ ἐξουσία	authority, power
ἡ ζωή	life
ἡ ἡμέρα	day
ἡ καρδία	heart
ἡ κεφαλή	head
ἡ σοφία	wisdom
ἡ φωνή	voice, sound
ἡ ὥρα	hour

Preposition:

ἐν	(with dative) in, at, by

Exercises

A. Translate into English:

1. ἡ ἀρχὴ εἰρήνης ἄγει ἀγάπην τῆς δόξης.
2. αἱ φωναὶ ἀγάπης εἶχον ἐξουσίαν καὶ σοφίαν.

3. ἡ βασιλεία τῆς ζωῆς ἦγεν τὰς ἡμέρας εἰρήνης;

4. αἱ δόξαι τῆς ζωῆς ἀγάπης κρίνουσιν τὰς ἁμαρτίας τῶν ἡμερῶν.

5. αἱ φωναὶ ἐξουσίας ἐλάμβανον τὴν σοφίαν τῆς ὥρας;

6. αἱ κεφαλαὶ ἐξουσίας ἔσωζον τὴν βασιλείαν τῆς σοφίας καὶ ἤμελλον κηρύσσειν τὴν ὥραν ἀγάπης.

7. ἤθελον αἱ ἡμέραι τῆς σοφίας βλέπειν τὰς ζωὰς τῆς ἀγάπης;

B. Translate into Greek:

1. They were raising the kingdom of sin.

2. In the heart peace was about to judge the hour.

3. The hours of life are finding the beginning of wisdom.

4. The glories of the life of love were willing to lead the days of life.

5. The kingdom of glory was about to find the peace of the heart.

Lesson V

1. Present Middle/Passive Indicative

a. In English there are two voices, *active* and *passive.* These reflect the action of the verb in relation to the subject of the sentence: In the active, the subject *acts;* e.g., "John hit the ball." In the passive, the subject is *acted upon;* e.g., "The ball was hit by John." The Greek language has these two voices, but in addition there is a third voice, the *middle.* This voice represents the subject as acting with reference to him/herself, either directly or indirectly. (Whether direct or indirect is determined by the verb and the context.) The *direct middle* would be translated "John is washing himself." The *indirect middle* would be translated "I am asking (buying, etc.) 'something' *for* myself." In each case the subject is acting with reference to oneself. Note carefully that this is *not* an intensive use of the reflexive in English. The middle is *predicative*, not nominative or adjectival — *not* "I myself am buying."

b. In some cases, however, there is a complete change of meaning from the active to the middle, e.g., active ἄρχω, to rule; middle ἄρχομαι, to begin. These changes must be learned for each verb from usage and vocabulary. In such cases the "myself," etc., component is no longer a part of the translation.

c. In the present system the middle and passive have identical endings. The context will determine which meaning is to be used in translation and interpretation.

d. The present middle and passive indicative is formed by finding the present tense stem (λύω→λυ-) and adding the following endings:

23

	Singular	**Plural**
1st person	-ομαι	-ομεθα
2nd person	-η	-εσθε
3rd person	-εται	-ονται

Infinitive -εσθαι

λύομαι	I am loosing myself (middle); I am being loosed (passive)	λυόμεθα
λύη		λύεσθε
λύεται		λύονται

Infinitive λύεσθαι

Again it must be emphasized that nothing short of mastery of these endings can suffice. These endings will be used again in different settings.

e. The imperfect middle and passive indicative is formed by finding the present stem, adding the augment (see Lesson III c), and adding the following endings:

	Singular	**Plural**
1st person	-ομην	-ομεθα
2nd person	-ου	-εσθε
3rd person	-ετο	-οντο

ἐλυόμην	I was loosing myself (middle); I was being loosed (passive)	ἐλυόμεθα
ἐλύου		ἐλύεσθε
ἐλύετο		ἐλύοντο

2. Agency

With the passive voice ὑπό may be used with the genitive to express agency (usually personal agents).

σώζομαι ὑπὸ τοῦ κυρίου (the lord).
I am being saved by the lord.

The dative of instrument is generally used to express impersonal means.

σώζομαι τῇ σοφίᾳ τῆς ἡμέρας.
I am being saved by the wisdom of the day.

Vocabulary

Verbs:

ἁμαρτάνω	sin
ἀναβαίνω	go up
ἀποθνῄσκω	die
βάλλω	throw, cast
διδάσκω	teach
διώκω	pursue, persecute
δοξάζω	glorify
κράζω	cry out
μένω	remain, abide
πείθω	persuade
χαίρω	rejoice

Preposition:

ὑπό   (with genitive) by; (with accusative) under

Exercises

A. Translate into English:

1. ἡ σοφία τῆς βασιλείας ἐδιδάσκετο τῇ ζωῇ εἰρήνης.
2. ἐβαπτίζοντο ἐξουσίᾳ;
3. σώζεται ὑπὸ τοῦ κυρίου (the lord) τῆς δόξης.
4. χαίρεις τῇ καρδίᾳ καὶ μένετε τῇ ἀγάπῃ.

5. ἐδιδάσκετο τὴν σοφίαν τῆς ὥρας καὶ ἐδιώκετο ὑπὸ τῆς βασιλείας τῆς ἁμαρτίας.

6. ἐπείθεσθε ὑπὸ τῆς σοφίας τῆς καρδίας, καὶ κράζει φωνῇ τῆς ἐξουσίας;

7. ἀποθνῄσκουσιν ἐν ταῖς ἁμαρτίαις τῆς κεφαλῆς καὶ τῆς καρδίας.

B. Translate into Greek:

1. He was glorifying himself. They are being glorified. You were being persecuted. We are being thrown.

2. They are about to be saved by the voice of the heart.

3. He was being heard by the lord of the kingdom of glory.

4. The power of the beginning of the sin was being cast by the power of love and wisdom.

5. Were the voices of love being heard by the lord of life?

LESSON VI

1. Second Declension Nouns

a. The second declension, or o-stem, contains primarily masculine and neuter nouns. The masculine nouns end in -ος and have the masculine definite article ὁ. The neuter nouns end in -ον and have the neuter definite article τό.

b. There are not different "types" of second declension nouns as there were in the first declension.

c. Endings for second declension nouns are as follows:

Masculine

	Singular	Plural
Nom.	-ος	-οι
Gen.	-ου	-ων
Dat.	-ῳ	-οις
Acc.	-ον	-ους
Voc.	-ε	-οι

Neuter

	Singular	Plural
Nom.	-ον	-α
Gen.	-ου	-ων
Dat.	-ῳ	-οις
Acc.	-ον	-α
Voc.	-ον	-α

d. *The Masculine Definite Article*

	Singular	Plural
Nom.	ὁ	οἱ
Gen.	τοῦ	τῶν
Dat.	τῷ	τοῖς
Acc.	τόν	τούς

e. *The Neuter Definite Article*

	Singular	Plural
Nom.	τό	τά
Gen.	τοῦ	τῶν
Dat.	τῷ	τοῖς
Acc.	τό	τά

2. Representative Second Declension Nouns

Observe the changes in accent in the following examples.

Masculine

	Singular	Plural
Nom.	ὁ ἄνθρωπος	οἱ ἄνθρωποι
Gen.	τοῦ ἀνθρώπου	τῶν ἀνθρώπων
Dat.	τῷ ἀνθρώπῳ	τοῖς ἀνθρώποις
Acc.	τὸν ἄνθρωπον	τοὺς ἀνθρώπους
Voc.	ἄνθρωπε	ἄνθρωποι

	Singular	Plural
Nom.	ὁ δοῦλος	οἱ δοῦλοι
Gen.	τοῦ δούλου	τῶν δούλων
Dat.	τῷ δούλῳ	τοῖς δούλοις
Acc.	τὸν δοῦλον	τοὺς δούλους
Voc.	δοῦλε	δοῦλοι

Masculine

	Singular	Plural
Nom.	ὁ οὐρανός	οἱ οὐρανοί
Gen.	τοῦ οὐρανοῦ	τῶν οὐρανῶν
Dat.	τῷ οὐρανῷ	τοῖς οὐρανοῖς
Acc.	τὸν οὐρανόν	τοὺς οὐρανούς
Voc.	οὐρανέ	οὐρανοί

Neuter

	Singular	Plural
Nom.	τὸ ἔργον	τὰ ἔργα
Gen.	τοῦ ἔργου	τῶν ἔργων
Dat.	τῷ ἔργῳ	τοῖς ἔργοις
Acc.	τὸ ἔργον	τὰ ἔργα
Voc.	ἔργον	ἔργα

a. Note that in the neuter the nominative and accusative singular are identical, as are the nominative and accusative plural. The *context* must determine which case is intended.

b. In Greek the neuter plural subject usually takes a singular verb. A group of "things" can be considered a single entity.

τὰ τέκνα ἄγει εἰς τὸν οἶκον.
The children are going into the house.

Vocabulary

Nouns:

ὁ ἄνθρωπος*	man
ὁ ἀπόστολος	apostle
ὁ ἄρτος	bread, loaf
ὁ διδάσκαλος	teacher

ὁ δοῦλος	slave
τὸ ἔργον	work
ὁ θάνατος	death
ὁ θεός	God
τὸ ἱερόν	temple
ὁ κύριος	lord, master
ὁ οἶκος	house
ὁ οὐρανός	heaven
τὸ πλοῖον	boat
τὸ σάββατον	Sabbath
τὸ τέχνον	child
ὁ φίλος	friend
ὁ χριστός	Christ, Messiah

*The word ἄνθρωπος may denote a specific "man," i.e., male, but it generally is used in the Greek language as "generic": singular = a person; plural = people, persons, including females as well as males.

Exercises

A. Translate into English:

1. οἱ ἄρτοι ἠσθίοντο τῷ σαββάτῳ.
2. ὁ θεὸς σώζει τὰ τέχνα ἀνθρώπων.
3. τῷ ἱερῷ ἡ βασιλεία τοῦ θεοῦ ἐδοξάζετο ὑπὸ τῶν δούλων εἰρήνης.
4. τὸ ἔργον τοῦ διδασκάλου ἐκηρύσσετο ὑπὸ τοῦ κυρίου τοῦ οἴκου.
5. διδάσκουσιν διδάσκαλοι τοῖς δούλοις τῆς σοφίας τὴν δόξαν ζωῆς;
6. οἱ ἄνθρωποι καὶ ἀπόστολοι ἔμενον καὶ ἐδιώκοντο ὑπὸ τῶν τέχνων τοῦ θανάτου καὶ τῶν φίλων τοῦ διδασκάλου;
7. τὰ πλοῖα ἄγεται ὑπὸ τοῦ ἔργου τοῦ ἀποστόλου.

B. Translate into Greek:

1. The work of sin is speaking to the children of wisdom.
2. The lord of the house was being taught by the apostles of death.
3. The beginning of wisdom is leading men in the life of heaven.
4. The slaves of the people were being heard by the lord of the house.

Lesson VII

1. Adjectives

a. Adjectives may be recognized in vocabulary lists because they do not have the definite article with them, and because they have the feminine and neuter nominative endings following the masculine.

$$\text{ἀγαθός, -η, -ον}$$

b. An adjective in Greek must agree with the noun it modifies in *gender, number,* and *case.* (Usually this means that the endings will be the same, but *not in every situation,* e.g., when the adjective follows the φωνή type and the noun the καρδία or δόξα type. Other combinations will be introduced later.)

c. There are two relationships which an adjective may have with a noun: *attributive* and *predicative.*

    i. The adjective may be related to the noun in the *attributive* position. That is, it immediately follows the definite article. This may be done in any one of three ways:

ὁ ἀγαθός δοῦλος	the good slave
ὁ δοῦλος ὁ ἀγαθός	the good slave
δοῦλος ὁ ἀγαθός	the good slave

    Of these, the first two are most commonly found, the third much less frequently.

    ii. The adjective may be related to the noun in the *predicative* position. That is, the adjective does not immediately follow the definite article.

32

ὁ δοῦλος ἀγαθός
or ἀγαθὸς ὁ δοῦλος   the slave is good

When the adjective is found in this position, the construction usually indicates a "nominal" sentence, in which the verb "to be" is understood.

In a nominal sentence, if there are two nouns, the one with the definite article is the subject (see Lesson VIII 2 a).

d. If there is no definite article (ἀγαθὸς δοῦλος or δοῦλος ἀγαθός), *context* must determine whether the adjective is attributive or predicative: either "a good slave" or "a slave is good."

e. *First and Second Declension Adjectives*

Singular

	Masculine	Feminine	Neuter
Nom.	ἀγαθός	ἀγαθή	ἀγαθόν
Gen.	ἀγαθοῦ	ἀγαθῆς	ἀγαθοῦ
Dat.	ἀγαθῷ	ἀγαθῇ	ἀγαθῷ
Acc.	ἀγαθόν	ἀγαθήν	ἀγαθόν
Voc.	ἀγαθέ	ἀγαθή	ἀγαθόν

Plural

	Masculine	Feminine	Neuter
Nom.	ἀγαθοί	ἀγαθαί	ἀγαθά
Gen.	ἀγαθῶν	ἀγαθῶν	ἀγαθῶν
Dat.	ἀγαθοῖς	ἀγαθαῖς	ἀγαθοῖς
Acc.	ἀγαθούς	ἀγαθάς	ἀγαθά
Voc.	ἀγαθοί	ἀγαθαί	ἀγαθά

Note that the endings are identical with the endings of the first and second declension nouns. Remember also that in adjective stems which end in -ε, -ι, or -ρ the feminine singular must follow the καρδία type of the first declension rather than the φωνή type. There is no δόξα type for the adjective.

f. The adjective may stand alone without any noun and be used as a noun.

οἱ ἀγαθοί   the good ones *or* the good people *or* the good men

2. Uses of αὐτός

αὐτός is a word that serves several purposes in the Greek language.

a. αὐτός is declined exactly like ἀγαθός except for the neuter nominative singular and the neuter accusative singular which have αὐτό rather than ἀυτόν.

b. *The Uses of* αὐτός

    i. αὐτός when used in the attributive position (directly following the article) means "same."

        ὁ αὐτὸς κύριος
        or ὁ κύριος ὁ αὐτός   the same master

    ii. When used in the *predicative* position, αὐτός usually means "self," corresponding to the English reflexive or intensive.

        ὁ κύριος αὐτός   the master himself

    When used in this way, the translation "myself," "yourself," or "himself" (and the corresponding plurals) is determined by the noun or pronoun which αὐτός modifies, since αὐτός has no person in itself when used as an adjective. It takes its "person" from the word it modifies.

    iii. When used *alone* in the oblique cases (genitive, dative, or accusative), however, αὐτός is the third person pronoun.

        διώκω αὐτόν   I am pursuing him
        λέγω αὐτῇ   I am speaking to her

ἐν τῷ ἔργῳ αὐτοῦ in the work of him, i.e., in
his work

ὁ κύριος αὐτῶν the master of them, i.e., their
master

3. Masculine Nouns of the First Declension; Feminine Nouns of the Second Declension

Studying the first and second declensions, one observes that usually the first declension nouns are feminine and the second declension nouns are either masculine or neuter. There are a few exceptions to this pattern, however.

a. There are several masculine nouns of the first declension. One can recognize these by noting that the definite article is masculine (ὁ) and that the nominative ending on the noun will be -ης or -ας (if the noun stem ends in -ε, -ι, or -ρ). When using an adjective with such a noun, remember that the adjective must agree with the noun in *gender*, number, and case, but not necessarily in ending.

Masculine

	Singular	Plural
Nom.	ὁ προφήτης	οἱ προφῆται
Gen.	τοῦ προφήτου	τῶν προφητῶν
Dat.	τῷ προφήτῃ	τοῖς προφήταις
Acc.	τὸν προφήτην	τοὺς προφήτας
Voc.	προφῆτα	προφῆται

Note that the nominative and genitive singular differ from the usual first declension nouns; otherwise the endings are the same.

Other nouns declined in this manner (except for accent) include ὁ μαθητής, disciple or learner; ὁ ὑποκριτής, hypocrite; ὁ νεανίας, youth.

b. There are a few feminine nouns of the second declension. These are declined with the usual second declension endings but with the feminine article. Note also that the adjective used with such a noun must be feminine.

ἡ ὁδός   the way, path, road

Feminine

	Singular	Plural
Nom.	ἡ ὁδός	αἱ ὁδοί
Gen.	τῆς ὁδοῦ	τῶν ὁδῶν
Dat.	τῇ ὁδῷ	ταῖς ὁδοῖς
Acc.	τὴν ὁδόν	τὰς ὁδούς

Another common noun of this category is ἡ ἔρημος, the desert, wilderness.

Vocabulary

Nouns:

ὁ ἀδελφός	brother
τὸ δῶρον	gift
ὁ μαθητής	disciple, learner
ὁ οἶνος	wine
ὁ προφήτης	prophet

Adjectives:

ἀγαθός, -η, -ον	good
ἀγαπητός, -η, -ον	beloved
αὐτός, -η, -ο	same, self
δίκαιος, -α, -ον	righteous
ἔσχατος, -η, -ον	last
κακός, -η, -ον	evil
καλός, -η, -ον	good, beautiful

μικρός, -α, -ον   small
μόνος, -η, -ον   only, alone
πιστός, -η, -ον   faithful
πονηρός, -α, -ον   evil
πρῶτος, -η, -ον   first

Exercises

A. Translate into English:

1. δίκαιος ὁ ἀδελφὸς τῆς σοφίας;
2. αἱ αὐταὶ κακαὶ ἁμαρτίαι λέγονται τῷ πιστῷ ὑπὸ τοῦ προφήτου αὐτοῦ.
3. ὁ ἔσχατος μαθητὴς δοξάζεται ἐν τῷ καλῷ ἱερῷ ὑπὸ τοῦ ἀδελφοῦ αὐτοῦ.
4. οἱ ἀγαθοὶ διδάσκονται ὑπὸ τῶν αὐτῶν μαθητῶν· μικραὶ πονηραὶ φωναὶ λέγουσιν τοῖς πιστοῖς.
5. οἱ κακοὶ ἄνθρωποι ἄγουσιν τοὺς ἀγαπητοὺς μαθητὰς ἐν τῇ ὁδῷ εἰρήνης καὶ ἀγάπης.
6. ὁ ἀγαπητὸς διδάσκαλος λαμβάνεται ἐν τῷ καλῷ ἱερῷ ὑπὸ τῶν ἀγαθῶν.
7. οἱ ἄρτοι καὶ ὁ οἶνος ἠσθίοντο τῷ σαββάτῳ ὑπὸ τῶν τέκνων τῶν δικαίων προφητῶν.

B. Translate into Greek:

1. The small child was being led by the good apostles.
2. The last gift is being taken by the teacher himself.
3. His house is rejoicing in the lord of life.
4. The gift itself was being received in the house of the faithful people.

LESSON VIII

1. Personal Pronouns (First and Second)

a. *First Person Pronoun*

	Singular		**Plural**	
Nom.	ἐγώ	I	ἡμεῖς	we
Gen.	ἐμοῦ, μου	of me	ἡμῶν	of us
Dat.	ἐμοί, μοι	to me, for me	ἡμῖν	to us, for us
Acc.	ἐμέ, με	me	ἡμᾶς	us

b. *Second Person Pronoun*

	Singular		**Plural**	
Nom.	σύ	you	ὑμεῖς	you
Gen.	σοῦ, σου	of you	ὑμῶν	of you
Dat.	σοί, σοι	to you, for you	ὑμῖν	to you, for you
Acc.	σέ, σε	you	ὑμᾶς	you

Note that the forms μου, μοι, με, σου, σοι, and σε are enclitic (see below) and that they are the most common forms in Greek writing. The longer forms are usually used for emphasis.

2. Present Tense of εἰμί

All present indicative tense forms of the verb εἰμί ("to be") are enclitic (see below) except the second person singular and the infinitive.

38

	Singular	**Plural**
1st person	εἰμί	ἐσμέν
2nd person	εἶ	ἐστέ
3rd person	ἐστί(ν)	εἰσί(ν)

Infinitive   εἶναι

a. The verb "to be" in Greek, as in English, takes a predicate nominative or adjective. It is not always necessary to include a form of the verb "to be" in a Greek sentence; the verb may simply be understood from the context. In such a sentence, the predicate nominative may be placed first for emphasis. A simple rule for determining the subject will be this: The subject usually has the article.

προφήτης ὁ ἀδελφός   The brother is a prophet.

If there is no article with either of the nouns, the context must determine which is the subject.

3. Enclitics

a. There are words in Greek which have no accent of their own and are called *enclitic* because they "lean in," i.e., lean back, on the preceding word and thus are pronounced with the preceding word. Since the accentuation patterns in Greek are centered on the last three syllables, certain changes are necessitated when an enclitic follows any other word. The accentuation of these combinations will depend, of course, on the accentuation of the preceding word.

b. There are both monosyllabic (one-syllable) and disyllabic (two-syllable) enclitics (see below).

c. The following rules will illustrate the possibilities.

i. If the preceding word has an accent on the antepenult, that word receives an additional acute on the ultima. This acute will *not* change to a grave.

ὁ ἀπόστολός μου or ὁ ἀπόστολός ἐστιν

ii. If the preceding word has an accent on the penult:

1. If that accent is a circumflex, the word receives an additional acute on the ultima.

ὁ δοῦλός μου

2. If the accent is acute:

a. If the enclitic is monosyllabic, the preceding word receives no additional accent.

ὁ λόγος μου

b. If the enclitic is disyllabic, the enclitic receives an acute on the ultima.

ὁ λόγος ἐστίν

iii. If the preceding word has an accent on the ultima: If the accent is a circumflex or an acute, it remains such no matter if the enclitic is mono- or disyllabic. There is some difference of opinion here, however, but this is the usually accepted consensus.

ὁ οὐρανός μου or οὐρανοῦ ἐστιν

d. If an enclitic is preceded by a proclitic (a word having no accent of its own which is pronounced with the following word, e.g., ἡ, αἱ, ὁ, οἱ, ἐχ, etc.) or another enclitic, the first of these will receive an acute on the ultima.

μού ἐστιν

e. ἐστί is written ἔστι in the following instances:

i. At the beginning of a sentence.
ii. When it immediately follows οὐχ, μή, εἰ, ὡς, χαί, ἀλλά, τοῦτο.
iii. When it means "exist" or "be possible."

These rules should be learned, but the solidification of the rules in the minds of those studying Greek will come more quickly if they will *carefully* observe their application in the exercises.

4. Prepositions Ending with a Vowel

When a preposition ends in a short vowel (as ἀπό), if the following word begins with a vowel or diphthong, that vowel will drop out.

$$\text{ἀπ' αὐτοῦ}$$

If the breathing on the following word is rough, certain letters—namely, π, χ, τ—will aspirate: π becomes φ; χ becomes χ; and τ becomes θ.

$$\text{ἀπ' ἡμέρας becomes ἀφ' ἡμέρας}$$

Vocabulary

Verbs:

ἀποστέλλω	send, send out
εἰμί	to be
εἰσάγω	go into, enter
ἐκβάλλω	cast out

Nouns:

ὁ ἄγγελος	messenger, angel
ἡ ἀλήθεια	truth
ἡ δικαιοσύνη	righteousness
ὁ κόσμος	world
ὁ νόμος	law
ὁ ὄχλος	crowd
τὸ ποτήριον	cup
ὁ υἱός	son
ὁ χρόνος	time
ἡ ψυχή	life, life principle

Pronouns:
ἐγώ   I
σύ   you

Negative Particle:
οὐ   not; οὐκ before smooth breathing;
        οὐχ before rough breathing

Prepositions:
ἀπό   from, away from (with genitive)
εἰς   into (with accusative)
ἐκ   out of, from within (with genitive);
        ἐξ before a vowel or diphthong

Conjunction:
ἀλλά   but

Exercises

A. Translate into English:

1. ἄγγελος ὁ κύριος ζωῆς;
2. ὁ δοῦλος χριστοῦ ἐστιν ἄνθρωπος δικαιοσύνης.
3. οἱ διδάσκαλοι ἐν τῷ ἱερῷ οὐκ ἐξέβαλλον τοὺς κακούς.
4. ὁ ἀδελφός μου ἀποστέλλεται εἰς τὸν κόσμον ὑπὸ τοῦ υἱοῦ σου.
5. οἱ νόμοι ἡμῶν ἄγουσιν τὰ τέκνα ὑμῶν εἰς τοὺς οἴκους ἁμαρτίας.
6. εἰ τέκνον τῆς βασιλείας ἀλλὰ φίλος ἁμαρτίας οὐκ ἔστιν υἱὸς τῆς ἀληθείας.
7. ἡ δόξα σου γράφεται ἐν τῷ νόμῳ ἀλλὰ ἡ ἁμαρτία αὐτῶν κηρύσσεται ὑπὸ τοῦ ἀποστόλου αὐτοῦ ἐν τῷ ἱερῷ τῆς καρδίας σου.

B. Translate into Greek:

1. We are children of God, but you are disciples of the world.
2. Are you (pl.) about to cast out the apostles of death?
3. My laws are being heard in the world by the messengers of truth.
4. Your (pl.) children are being seen by our slaves.

LESSON IX

1. Deponent Verbs

There are some verbs in Greek which have no active forms, only middle and/or passive forms, but are translated actively. These verbs are called deponent (because they have "laid aside" the active endings). They are listed in the vocabulary lists in the first person singular middle/passive form, e.g., ἔρχομαι, I come, go.

All forms of these verbs based on the present tense verb stem will be deponent; the imperfect is the only system studied thus far which is based on the present stem.

2. Demonstrative Pronouns

a. In Greek there are two demonstrative pronouns: οὗτος, this; and ἐκεῖνος, that. οὗτος is declined as follows:

Singular

	Masculine	**Feminine**	**Neuter**
Nom.	οὗτος	αὕτη	τοῦτο
Gen.	τούτου	ταύτης	τούτου
Dat.	τούτῳ	ταύτῃ	τούτῳ
Acc.	τοῦτον	ταύτην	τοῦτο

Plural

	Masculine	**Feminine**	**Neuter**
Nom.	οὗτοι	αὗται	ταῦτα
Gen.	τούτων	τούτων	τούτων
Dat.	τούτοις	ταύταις	τούτοις
Acc.	τούτους	ταύτας	ταῦτα

44

b. Note the first and second declension endings.

c. Note also the *o*-vowel in the stem when the final vowel (vowel of the ending) is ο, and the *a*-vowel in the stem when the final vowel is α or η.

d. ἐκεῖνος is declined exactly like αὐτός (see Lesson VII) except for the accent. It is identical in endings to the first and second declension adjectives except for the neuter nominative and accusative singular, where ἐκεῖνο is found.

e. When the demonstrative is used with a noun, the noun must have the article, and the demonstrative is in the *predicative* position.

οὗτος ὁ κόσμος   this world
τὴν βασιλείαν ταύτην   this kingdom

When the construction is οὗτος λόγος, the proper translation is "this is a word," not "this word."

f. The demonstrative may also stand alone (compare the use of adjectives).

οὗτος   this man *or* this one
τοῦτο   this thing
ταῦτα   these things
ἐκεῖνα   those things

3. Conditional Sentences (First Class Conditional)

a. In the Greek language there is a sentence construction in which there is a subordinate clause (called the protasis) which sets forth a premise, and a main clause (called the apodosis) which defines the result of that premise. In a conditional sentence the protasis is assumed to be fulfilled or unfulfilled.

b. There are four types of these sentences. The first is the condition that is *determined as fulfilled,* called the first class condition. In this the protasis makes a statement assumed to be true (it may or may not be true in actuality) for the purpose of the particular argument.

The pattern for this type of condition is as follows:

Protasis	Apodosis
εἰ + a verb in the indicative mode	a verb in any mode or tense

εἰ οὗτος ἐστιν δίκαιος,
    ἀγόμεθα ὑπὸ τοῦ λόγου τοῦ θεοῦ.
If this one is just,
    we are being led by the word of God.

Note that the conditional clause is stated as if it were a fact; that is, "this one" may or may not in reality be "just"—but for the purpose of this statement it is *assumed* to be true.

c. Because of this, the εἰ may be translated in certain contexts by the causal "since." Since this one is just, we are being led by the word of God.

The student is advised here to make a chart of the conditional sentences to which the patterns and definitions for the other three may be added at the appropriate time. This can be of great benefit to students if they will do this and refer to the chart frequently.

Vocabulary

Verbs:

γίνομαι	be, become, happen
ἔρχομαι	go, come
συνάγω	gather together

Nouns:

ἡ ἀσθένεια	weakness, sickness
ἡ ἐντολή	commandment
ὁ θρόνος	throne
τὸ ἱμάτιον	garment
ἡ κώμη	village

ὁ λαός	people
ὁ λίθος	stone
ὁ λόγος	word, reason
ὁ μισθός	pay, wages
ὁ ὀφθαλμός	eye
ἡ συναγωγή	assembly, gathering
ὁ τόπος	place
ἡ χαρά	joy

Adjectives:

ἐκεῖνος, -η, -ο	that (one)
ἕτερος, -α, -ον	other
οὗτος, αὕτη, τοῦτο	this (one)

Preposition:

σύν	with (with dative)

Conjunction:

εἰ	if

Exercises

A. Translate into English:

1. αὗται αἱ κῶμαι εὑρίσκονται ὑπὸ τῶν κυρίων ἐκείνων;
2. ἡ ἐντολὴ τῆς χαρᾶς κηρύσσεται ὑπὸ ἐκείνων ἐν τῷ ἱερῷ καὶ τῇ συναγωγῇ.
3. εἰ ὑμεῖς διδάσκετε τὸν λαόν, οὗτοι οἱ ἀγαθοὶ προφῆται μέλλουσιν λαμβάνειν τὴν δόξαν.
4. ἐκεῖνοι ἄγουσιν τοὺς υἱοὺς τούτους εἰς τὴν συναγωγὴν τῆς ἁμαρτίας.
5. εἰ οἱ ἀπόστολοι αὐτοὶ ἤρχοντο εἰς τὸν οἶκον τοῦτον, ἡ βασιλεία τῆς δόξης γίνεται ἐξουσία ἐν τῷ τόπῳ τούτῳ.
6. εἰ ἡμεῖς κηρύσσομεν τὸν κύριον, ἄγομεν τοὺς δούλους ἐκείνους εἰς τὴν σοφίαν τῆς ὥρας ἐκείνης.

B. Translate into Greek:

1. Those evil prophets were being pursued by the sons of that village.
2. Is this man finding his sons in the temple?
3. If we are finding the words of life, we are proclaiming those words in the place of the heart.
4. These loaves were being eaten by the men of that village.

LESSON X

1. Subjunctive Mood

The subjunctive mood in Greek basically expresses doubt or hesitancy. It is the "contingency" mood. There is no general formula by which to translate the subjunctive into English because each subjunctive construction comes over into English in its own particular way. The appropriate translation must be learned for each construction. One must note well that the main verb in the main clause of the sentence cannot be in the subjunctive mood *except in specialized constructions*. In Greek one does *not* find expressions such as "I may go to town" as the main clause in the sentence!

2. Present Subjunctive

a. The Verb "to be"

	Singular	Plural
1st person	ὦ	ὦμεν
2nd person	ᾖς	ἦτε
3rd person	ᾖ	ὦσι(ν)

b. To form the present active subjunctive of a verb one must find the present stem (λύω→λυ-) and add the following endings:

	Singular	**Plural**
1st person	-ω	-ωμεν
2nd person	-ης	-ητε
3rd person	-η	-ωσι(ν)

λύω	λύωμεν
λύῃς	λύητε
λύῃ	λύωσι(ν)

Note (1) the similarity of endings here to the forms of the verb "to be" above; (2) the recessive accent; and (3) the lengthening of the connecting vowel(s).

The negative with non-indicative is μή.

c. To form the present middle/passive subjunctive of a verb one follows the same procedure as in forming the present active subjunctive, but the following endings are added to the present stem:

	Singular	**Plural**
1st person	-ωμαι	-ωμεθα
2nd person	-ῃ	-ησθε
3rd person	-ηται	-ωνται

λύωμαι	λυώμεθα
λύῃ	λύησθε
λύηται	λύωνται

3. Uses of the Subjunctive

a. The subjunctive is used in subordinate clauses after certain conjunctions, e.g., ἵνα. ὅπως

> ἄγομεν ἵνα βλέπωμεν αὐτόν
> We are going in order that we may see him.

The auxiliary verb here for the proper English translation is "may" (or "might").

b. The subjunctive is used as the main verb in the sentence in specialized constructions:

     i. The *cohortative* (or hortatory) subjunctive. In such cases the verb will be in the first person plural, subjunctive mood, and will be the main verb in the main clause.

        διώκωμεν τὰ τέκνα τῆς σοφίας
        Let us persecute (*or* pursue) the children of wisdom.

     Since the present tense indicates primarily *kind of action* and in the non-indicative moods usually has very little to do with "time" per se, a better translation of this sentence would be "Let us continue to persecute (*or* keep on persecuting) the children of wisdom."

     ii. The subjunctive is used in either the first person singular or the first person plural, subjunctive mood, when the speaker asks a question and expects some answer from those addressed. This is called the *deliberative* subjunctive. (This is really the interrogative counterpart of the cohortative.)

        ἄγωμεν εἰς τὸν οἶκον;
        Shall we go into the house?

c. There are numerous other usages of the subjunctive mood both in subordinate clauses and in other special ways. These will be introduced at appropriate points as the grammar progresses. It is highly advisable to make a chart listing the various usages of the subjunctive mood. When each new construction is introduced, it can easily be added to the list.

Vocabulary

Verbs:

ἀνοίγω	open
ἀσπάζομαι	salute
βασιλεύω	reign
δέχομαι	receive
δουλεύω	serve (as a slave) (with dative)
ἐλπίζω	hope
θαυμάζω	marvel, wonder
θεραπεύω	heal
καθαρίζω	purify
καταλύω	destroy
νομίζω	think, suppose
πειράζω	test, put to the test
σύρω	drag, draw
ὑπάγω	go away, depart

Adverbs:

μή	not; used with non-indicative moods
πῶς	how? (interrogative)

Conjunction:

ἵνα	in order that (with the subjunctive)

Exercises

A. Translate into English:

1. ἐλπίζωμεν ἵνα ἡ δικαιοσύνη τοῦ θεοῦ βασιλεύῃ ἐν τῷ κόσμῳ.
2. ὁ αὐτὸς προφήτης ἀσπάζεται ἵνα γινώμεθα δοῦλοι τῆς ἀληθείας.
3. πῶς ὦμεν ἀγαθοί;
4. ὁ νόμος μου πειράζει τὴν ἀσθένειαν τοῦ κακοῦ ὀφθαλμοῦ.

5. ἐρχώμεθα ἵνα ἡ συναγωγὴ θαυμάζῃ καὶ θεραπεύηται.
6. ὁ μαθητὴς καθαρίζεται ἵνα μὴ μένωσιν ἐν τῇ ἁμαρτίᾳ.
7. ἐγὼ ὑπάγω ἵνα λύησθε ὑπὸ τοῦ δούλου αὐτοῦ.
8. εἰ καθαρίζει τὰς ψυχὰς τῶν ἀνθρώπων, ὑπάγωμεν ἀφ᾽ ἁμαρτίας.

B. Translate into Greek:

1. Let us be good people in order that the same lord may heal the sins of the world.
2. How shall we be saved?
3. We are saluting in order that the righteousness of God may purify the weaknesses of the apostles.
4. Let us continue to serve the lord of life in order that the evil people of the world may see the truth of God.

Lesson XI

1. Future Principal Part of Verbs

a. As in English, the Greek verb has principal parts; but whereas the verb in English has three parts, the verb in Greek has six! The first person singular present active indicative constitutes the first principal part, e.g., λύω. The second principal part is the future active indicative. The remaining four principal parts will be introduced in the chapters immediately following. (Each principal part will be in the first person singular.)

b. The regular way of forming the future tense is as follows:

    i. Find the verb stem by removing the -ω from the present tense form: λύω→λυ-. [Note that the *verb* stem is not always the same as the present stem. This will be learned by observation and by consulting the lexicon.]

    ii. Next the stem receives a -σ- as a suffix: λυσ-.

    iii. To this form are added the same endings that have already been learned for the present active indicative.

The future tense is translated as in English and carries the same intent as in English.

c. *The Future Active Indicative*

Singular		Plural	
λύσω	I shall loose	λύσομεν	we shall loose
λύσεις	you will loose	λύσετε	you will loose
λύσει	he, she, it will loose	λύσουσι(ν)	they will loose

54

Conjunction:

ἐάν   if (with subjunctive)

Exercises

A. Translate into English:

1. ἐὰν ἁγιάζησθε, κηρύξετε τὴν σοφίαν τοῦ θεοῦ.
2. ἄξω τοὺς υἱοὺς τῆς βασιλείας εἰς τὸν οἶκον τοῦ κακοῦ.
3. ὁ κύριος σώζει τοὺς ἀγαθοὺς καὶ ἐλεύσονται (deponent future of ἔρχομαι) εἰς τὴν βασιλείαν.
4. διώξουσιν καὶ ἁγιάσουσιν ἐκείνους ἵνα ὁ θεὸς χαίρῃ.
5. ἐὰν δέχωνται τὰ δῶρα ἡμῶν, ἐγγίσομεν εἰς τὸ ἱερὸν αὐτοῦ;
6. καταβαίνωμεν ἵνα σκανδαλίζωμεν τοὺς κακοὺς τούτους.
7. ἐὰν χρονίζῃς ἐν τῷ οἴκῳ τοῦ κυρίου, οἱ ἀγαθοὶ διώξουσιν τὰς ὁδοὺς τῆς δικαιοσύνης.

B. Translate into Greek:

1. If the sons of evil would pursue the wisdom of God, they will draw near to the kingdom of God.
2. These men will shake the heavens and the temple, and those women will begin to proclaim the lives of the good prophets.
3. Let us continue to pursue the ways of the righteousness of God.
4. If the slaves of wisdom would receive the kingdom, the world will proclaim truth and peace.

LESSON XII

1. First Aorist Principal Part of Verbs

a. The *aorist* tense forms the third principal part of the Greek verb. [It is the first person singular aorist active indicative that is found as the third principal part.] The word "aorist" means "not determined" or "undefined"; that is, a statement is made about the action, but the action itself is not described.

b. The aorist indicative indicates undefined action in past time; therefore, this form will have the augment (see Lesson III 1 c).

c. There are two kinds of aorist stems, the first aorist and the second aorist. The *first aorist* is formed in the following manner. The verb stem is found (λύω→λυ-). To this is prefixed the temporal augment ἐ-; a -σ- is then added as a suffix (as in the future). The same consonantal changes will occur as with the future (see Lesson X 1 e). The following endings are then added:

Active

	Singular	Plural
1st person	-α	-αμεν
2nd person	-ας	-ατε
3rd person	-ε(ν)	-αν

Infinitive   -αι

Middle

	Singular	Plural
1st person	-αμην	-αμεθα
2nd person	-ω	-ασθε
3rd person	-ατο	-αντο

Infinitive -ασθαι

d. The conjugation of the aorist active and middle indicatives is as follows:

Active

	Singular		Plural
ἔλυσα	I loosed	ἐλύσαμεν	we loosed
ἔλυσας	you loosed	ἐλύσατε	you (pl.) loosed
ἔλυσε(ν)	he, she, it loosed	ἔλυσαν	they loosed

Infinitive λῦσαι to loose

Middle

	Singular		Plural
ἐλυσάμην	I loosed for myself	ἐλυσάμεθα	we loosed for ourselves
ἐλύσω	you loosed for yourself	ἐλύσασθε	you loosed for yourselves
ἐλύσατο	he, she, it loosed for him-, her-, itself	ἐλύσαντο	they loosed for themselves

Infinitive λύσασθαι to loose for oneself

Note that the first aorist infinitive is accented on the penult in the active, but normally (i.e., with a recessive accent) in the middle.

e. In Greek the imperfect and aorist tenses both indicate action in past time. The difference between the aorist and the imperfect is in the *kind of action* indicated—

undefined versus *linear*. "The man was reading (*or* continued to read) the book"—imperfect. "The man read the book"—aorist.

2. Infinitive and Subjunctive of Aorist Verbs

a. The non-indicative modes of the aorist have no augment. In these usages the aorist denotes *kind of action*. For example, the aorist infinitive denotes undefined action. The present infinitive denotes continued or repeated action.

λύειν to be (keep) loosing
λῦσαι to loose

b. The subjunctive mood of the first aorist is formed by removing from the aorist principal part the augment and the ending (ελυσα→λυσ- [aorist stem]) and by adding the same endings used to form the present subjunctive active and middle.

Active

Singular	Plural
λύσω	λύσωμεν
λύσῃς	λύσητε
λύσῃ	λύσωσι(ν)

Middle

Singular	Plural
λύσωμαι	λυσώμεθα
λύσῃ	λύσησθε
λύσηται	λύσωνται

Note that the forms which are identical with other tenses and moods must be distinguished *by the context*.

Note also that the aorist subjunctive is translated quite similarly to the present subjunctive, but there is a difference of meaning, namely, kind of action.

ἵνα λύσῃ in order that he may loose
ἵνα λύῃ in order that he may keep on loosing

3. Postpositive Particles

A postpositive particle is given in the vocabulary, δέ. Postpositive means that the word cannot stand as the first element in a sentence or clause. It is usually placed second (or sometimes a word or two later), but this has no effect on determining, for instance, whether an adjective is attributive or not.

ὁ δὲ ἀγαθὸς λόγος but the good word . . .

Vocabulary

Verbs:

δεῖ	it is necessary (impersonal verb)
ἐπιστρέφω	turn, return
πίπτω	fall
προσεύχομαι	pray

Nouns:

ὁ ἄγρος	field
τὸ μνημεῖον	tomb
ὁ ναός	temple
ἡ χώρα	country

Adjective:

λοιπός, -η, -ον	remaining
νεκρός, -α, -ον	dead

Adverbs:

εὐθέως	immediately, straightway
μηκέτι	no longer

Preposition:

ἔμπροσθεν	before, in the presence of (with genitive; also used as an adverb)
περί	around (with genitive, dative, or accusative)

Interrogative:
    πότε   when?

Postpositive Particle:
    δέ   but, on the other hand

Exercises

A. Translate into English:

1. εἰ ἐδόξασας ταῦτα, οὐκ ἔσωσας αὐτούς.
2. ἤρξατο βαπτίσαι αὐτοὺς σὺν τοῖς τέκνοις αὐτῶν.
3. ἀγώμεθα ὑπὸ τοῦ υἱοῦ καὶ πιστεύσωμεν ἐν τῷ λόγῳ αὐτοῦ.
4. θέλει λύσασθαι ἵνα κηρύξῃ ἐν τῷ οἴκῳ τοῦ φίλου αὐτοῦ;
5. ἐδεξάμην τὸν δοῦλον, οἱ δὲ μαθηταὶ τῆς δόξης οὐκ ἤρχοντο πρός με.
6. ὁ αὐτὸς λόγος ἐδιδάσκετο ἐν τῷ ἱερῷ ὑπὸ τούτου ἵνα ἄνθρωποι βλέψωσι καὶ ἀκούσωσι καὶ γινώσκωσιν τὴν ἀλήθειαν τῆς βασιλείας τοῦ θεοῦ.
7. ἄξωμεν καὶ ἄγωμεν οἱ δίκαιοι τοῦ κόσμου τούτου πρὸς τὸν υἱόν.
8. ὁ δὲ κακὸς προφήτης ἐσάλευσεν τὰς ἡμέρας τῶν ἁμαρτιῶν;

B. Translate into Greek:

1. The slave of righteousness will see the lord in order that his sons may also see him.
2. Let us be led by the God of truth and wisdom.
3. If you baptized the children, the evil prophets glorified the law.
4. Shall we loose the children of truth in order that the good people of this world may spend time in the temple?

LESSON XIII

1. Second Aorist Principal Part of Verbs

a. Not all verbs have a first aorist form. Some have what is known as the *second aorist*. This particular part of the Greek verbal system is the oldest form of the verb. It is distinguished generally by a weakening of the vowel in the stem of the verb. It is almost impossible to predict what kind of change will occur, however, for many times the second aorist is built on a different verb stem altogether from the present stem. The second aorist is a "strong" form analogous to strong verb forms in English. For example, "go, went, gone" (strong); "learn, learned, learned" (weak).

b. Since the second aorist is a secondary tense (action in the past) one will expect to find an augment. The endings for the second aorist are identical with those of the imperfect.

Active

	Singular	Plural
1st person	-ον	-ομεν
2nd person	-ες	-ετε
3rd person	-ε(ν)	-ον

Infinitive   -ειν

ἦλθον	I came, went	ἤλθομεν	we came
ἦλθες	you came	ἤλθετε	you (pl.)came
ἦλθε(ν)	he, she, it came	ἦλθον	they came

Infinitive   ἐλθεῖν   to come

63

Middle

	Singular	Plural
1st person	-ομην	-ομεθα
2nd person	-ου	-εσθε
3rd person	-ετο	-οντο

Infinitive εσθαι

ἠλθόμην	ἠλθόμεθα
ἤλθου	ἤλθεσθε
ἤλθετο	ἤλθοντο

Infinitive ἐλθέσθαι

The accent on the second aorist active infinitive is a circumflex on the ultima.

The accent on the second aorist middle infinitive is an acute on the penult.

The aorist infinitive has no augment. The difference between the present infinitive and the aorist infinitive is *kind of action.*

λύειν to be loosing (to keep loosing, etc.)
ἐλθεῖν to come

2. Subjunctive of Second Aorist Verbs

a. To form the subjunctive one must find the aorist stem: ἤλθον→ελθ-. To this is added the *same* endings already learned in connection with the present and first aorist subjunctive.

Active

Singular	Plural
ἔλθω	ἔλθωμεν
ἔλθῃς	ἔλθητε
ἔλθῃ	ἔλθωσι(ν)

Middle*

ἔλθωμαι	ἐλθώμεθα
ἔλθῃ	ἔλθησθε
ἔλθηται	ἔλθωνται

*It should be noted that the middle forms of ἦλθον do not appear in the New Testament but are given here for illustrative purposes.

3. Imperfect of εἰμί

Conjugation of the imperfect active indicative of "to be":

Singular		**Plural**	
ἤμην (ἦν)	I was	ἦμεν, ἤμεθα	we were
ἦς, ἦσθα	you were	ἦτε	you (pl.)were
ἦν	he, she, it was	ἦσαν	they were

4. Conditional Sentences (Second Class Conditional)

a. There is another type of conditional sentence found in the Greek language called the Second Class Conditional. This condition is determined as *unfulfilled*. It is formed by utilizing the secondary (past) tenses. The second class conditional sentence may be either present or past. The pattern is as follows:

Protasis	**Apodosis**
Present: εἰ + a verb in the imperfect indicative	ἄν + a verb in the imperfect indicative
Past: εἰ + a verb in the aorist indicative	ἄν + a verb in the aorist (or pluperfect) indicative

b. The present second class conditional sentence is translated by using the present tense of the subjunctive in English: "If I were . . . , they would be . . . ."

εἰ ἔλυον τοὺς προφήτας, ἂν ἦσαν ἀγαθοὶ δοῦλοι
If they were loosing the prophets, they would be good slaves.

c. The past second class conditional sentence is translated by using the past tense of the subjunctive in English: "If I had been . . . , they would have been . . . .'

εἰ ἔλυσαν τοὺς προφήτας, ἂν ἐδούλευσαν τῷ κυρίῳ
If they had loosed the prophets, they would have served the lord.

d. Since the protasis is assumed to be unfulfilled, the apodosis cannot be true, hence the use of the modal particle ἄν. The ἄν is not really translated but gives modality or contingency to the construction, shown in English by our word "would."

The ἄν is normally used in second class conditional sentences, but there are instances where it does not appear, the context being assumed to be clear enough to make the use of the ἄν superfluous. Context must determine in some instances, therefore, whether a construction is first or second class conditional.

e. Since εἰμί does not have an aorist form, when a second class conditional sentence has the imperfect of εἰμί in one of the clauses, the tense of the entire construction must be determined by the verb in the other clause.

Present: εἰ τὸ τέχνον ἦν ἐν τῷ οἴχῳ, ἂν οἱ κακοὶ ἔλυον τοὺς δούλους.
If the child were in the house, the evil people would loose the slaves.

Past: εἰ τὸ τέχνον ἦν ἐν τῷ οἴχῳ, ἂν οἱ κακοὶ ἔλυσαν τοὺς δούλους.
If the child had (been) in the house, the evil people would have loosed the slaves.

Vocabulary

Verbs:

These forms are the second aorist principal parts of the verbs cited.

ἀπέθανον—ἀποθνῄσκω
ἔβαλον—βάλλω
ἐγενόμην—γίνομαι
εἶδον—ὁράω   see
εἶπον—λέγω
ἔλαβον—λαμβάνω
ἔλιπον—λείπω   leave
ἔπεσον—πίπτω
ἔσχον—ἔχω
ἔφαγον—ἐσθίω
ἦλθον—ἔρχομαι
εὗρον—εὑρίσκω

Exercises

A. Translate into English:

1. εὗρον τὸ ἱμάτιον ἵνα τὸ σάββατον μὴ πέσῃ εἰς κακόν.
2. εἰ ἦσαν ἐν τῷ τόπῳ τῆς χαρᾶς, ἂν οὐκ εἶδον τὴν ἁμαρτίαν ζωῆς.
3. ἐν συναγωγῇ ὁ λόγος ἐγένετο ἐξουσία καὶ ὁ λαὸς ἔφαγεν τὸν ἄρτον τοῦ ἱεροῦ ἵνα ἴδωσιν τὴν σοφίαν τῆς δόξης.
4. εἰ τὸ ἔργον τοῦ δούλου ἔλαβεν τὸν αὐτὸν μισθόν, ἂν ὁ φίλος οὐκ ἔβαλεν λίθους εἰς τὸν οἶκον τοῦ κυρίου.
5. ἐκεῖνοι ἔλαβον τὰ τέκνα ἐκ τοῦ οἴκου καὶ ἐδόξαζον τὸν θεόν.
6. εὕρωμεν τὴν σοφίαν ἵνα φάγωσιν τὸν ἄρτον τῆς ζωῆς;
7. εἶδον τὸν λόγον τῆς ζωῆς καὶ ἐκήρυσσον τὴν δικαιοσύνην τοῦ θεοῦ.

B. Translate into Greek:

1. If you had received the bread of life from the lord, you would have loosed the slaves of sin.
2. The children threw stones into the house of the master.
3. I found wisdom and love in the assembly of the good people in order that you (pl.) might eat the bread of life.
4. These women will loose the words of truth, and those men will save the children from sin.

Lesson XIV

1. Perfect Active Principal Part of Verbs

a. The fourth principal part of the Greek verb is the perfect tense. The perfect is usually translated by the present perfect in English (I have loosed, etc.), but the *kind of action* is somewhat more specific. Perfective action in Greek represents an act completed in the past with the results of that action still in force. This is sometimes difficult to bring out in translation. For example, the usual way of introducing an Old Testament quotation in the New Testament is by using the perfect tense of γράφω, i.e., γέγραπται: "it has been written," or "it stands written," or "it is written." The implication of the perfect tense here is evident.

b. The perfect tense is characterized by a *reduplication*. One finds the verb stem (λύω→λυ-). Then one "reduplicates" by prefixing a connecting -ε- and the initial consonant of the verb (λελυ-) and completes the tense form by adding a -κ- as a suffix (λελυκ-) and the following endings:

	Singular	Plural
1st person	-α	-αμεν
2nd person	-ας	-ατε
3rd person	-ε(ν)	-αν (or occasionally ασι)

Infinitive   -εναι

69

λέλυκα	I have loosed	λελύκαμεν	we have loosed
λέλυκας	you have loosed	λελύκατε	you (pl.) have loosed
λέλυκε(ν)	he, she, it has loosed	λέλυκαν	they have loosed

Infinitive   λελυκέναι   to loose or to have loosed

Note that the endings are identical to those of the first aorist (except for the infinitive, which is similar) and that the accent on the perfect active infinitive is on the penult.

c. In the reduplication process, when the initial letter of the verb is a vowel or diphthong or when the word begins with two or more consonants (one of which is usually a sibilant), a double consonant, or ρ-, the reduplication looks exactly like an augment.

$$ἐγγίζω → ἤγγικα$$
$$στέλλω → ἔσταλκα$$

Singular		Plural
ἔσταλκα	I have sent	ἐστάλκαμεν
ἔσταλκας	etc.	ἐστάλκατε
ἔσταλκε(ν)		ἔσταλκαν

Infinitive   ἐσταλκέναι   to send or to have sent

d. *Other Variations*
   i. When the verb stem ends in τ, δ, or θ, the τ, δ, or θ drops out before the addition of the κ: σώζω → σέσωκα.
   ii. When the initial consonant of the verb is φ, χ, or θ, the reduplication is made by the corresponding *hard* form, i.e., τ for θ, π for φ, κ for χ.

$$θεραπεύω → τεθεράπευκα$$
$$φιλέω \text{ (love) } → πεφίληκα$$

e. Not all perfect tense forms are "regular." There are some old "strong" forms (compare the second aorist) which do not follow the normal pattern. These forms must be learned for each verb.

Here are a few of the more important second perfects.

Present		*Second Perfect*
ἀκούω	hear	ἀκήκοα
γίνομαι	become	γέγονα
γινώσκω	know	ἔγνωκα
γράφω	write	γέγραφα
ἔρχομαι	come, go	ἐλήλυθα
ὁράω	see	ἑώρακα

2. Perfect Middle/Passive Principle Part of Verbs

The perfect middle/passive is the fifth principal part of the Greek verb. This form is usually patterned in the same manner as the perfect active with the exception of the -κ- (λελυ-). The middle/passive ending is added to the verb stem *with no connecting vowel.*

Perfect Middle/Passive

	Singular	**Plural**
1st person	-μαι	-μεθα
2nd person	-σαι	-σθε
3rd person	-ται	-νται

Infinitive   -σθαι

λέλυμαι	I have been loosed;	λελύμεθα
	I have loosed myself	
λέλυσαι	etc.	λέλυσθε
λέλυται		λέλυνται

Infinitive   λελύσθαι

3. Pluperfect Tense

a. There is a pluperfect tense in Greek which also expresses perfective action but in this case from one point in the past to another point in the past. The pluperfect is usually translated by the English past perfect tense (I had loosed). This tense is found very infrequently in the New Testament.

b. The pluperfect is formed on the perfect stem. Sometimes there will be an augment, but this is not always the case by this stage of the development of the Greek language.

Pluperfect Active Indicative

	Singular	Plural
1st person	-ειν	-ειμεν
2nd person	-εις	-ειτε
3rd person	-ει	-εισαν

(ἐ)λελύκειν	I had loosed	(ἐ)λελύκειμεν
(ἐ)λελύκεις	etc.	(ἐ)λελύκειτε
(ἐ)λελύκει		(ἐ)λελύκεισαν

Note that the connecting vowel in this tense is a diphthong—ει.

Vocabulary

Verbs:

ἀποκτείνω	kill
ἀπολύω	release
δύναμαι	be able
ἐπιγινώσκω	come to know, recognize
προσέρχομαι	come to
προσφέρω	bring to, offer

Nouns:

ἡ γραφή	writing, scripture
ὁ καρπός	fruit
τό σημεῖον	sign
ἡ φυλακή	guard, prison, watch

Adjectives:

ἅγιος, -α, -ον	holy
δεξιός, -α, -ον	right (opposite of left)
ἕκαστος, -η, -ον	each
ἕτοιμος, -η, -ον	prepared, ready
μακάριος, -α, -ον	happy, blessed

Adverbs:

ἄρα	then, therefore
ἤδη	now, already

Conjunction:

γάρ	for (postpositive particle)
ὅτι	that, because

Interrogative:

ποῦ	where? whither?

Exercises

A. Translate into English:

1. ὅτι ἑώρακάς με πεπίστευκας· μακάριοι ἐκεῖνοι οὐχ ἑώρακαν ἀλλὰ πιστεύουσιν.

2. γέγραπται ὅτι οὗτος ἐν τῇ δεξιᾷ τοῦ θεοῦ δύναται λελυκέναι τὰς ἁμαρτίας τοῦ κόσμου.

3. ἔγνωκαν τὸν κύριον τῆς δόξης καὶ ἑώρακαν τὴν ἐξουσίαν τοῦ λόγου αὐτοῦ.

4. ὁ χριστὸς τοῦ θεοῦ ἐλήλυθεν εἰς τὸν κόσμον καὶ ἡμεῖς πεπιστεύκαμεν ὅτι αὐτός ἐστιν ὁ ἅγιος τῆς δικαιοσύνης.

5. εἰ ἐπίστευσαν ἐν τῷ θεῷ τῆς γράφης, ἂν οὐκ ἀπέθανον ἐν ταῖς ἁμαρτίαις αὐτῶν.

6. ἐὰν βλέψωσιν τοὺς λόγους τῆς ζωῆς, οἱ ἄνθρωποι τῆς φυλακῆς ἐλεύσονται εἰς τὸν τόπον τῆς δικαιοσύνης.

B. Translate into Greek:

1. If you had seen the apostles of truth, you would not have come into the house of the evil men.
2. You have seen and heard and believed that the lord has the words of life.
3. It has been written that the Messiah will save the world from evil.
4. If the words of truth would be believed, these people will begin to find peace.

Lesson XV

1. Aorist Passive Principal Part of Verbs

a. The sixth (and last!) principal part of the Greek verb is the aorist passive. The aorist passive indicative is formed by finding the verb stem (λύω→λυ-), prefixing an augment ε- (ἐλυ-), adding a -θ- as a suffix (ἐλυθ-) and adding the following endings.

Aorist Passive Indicative

	Singular	Plural
1st person	-ην	-ημεν
2nd person	-ης	-ητε
3rd person	-η	-ησαν

Infinitive   -ηναι

ἐλύθην	I was loosed	ἐλύθημεν
ἐλύθης	etc.	ἐλύθητε
ἐλύθη		ἐλύθησαν

Infinitive   λυθῆναι   to be loosed

b. These are *active* endings on the aorist passive conjugation. Note also the similarity to the imperfect active endings.

c. The accent is on the penult of the infinitive.

d. When the -θ- is added to a verb stem as a suffix, there are several changes that occur with certain consonants. If the verb stem ends in π or β, those letters become φ.

λαμβάνω → ἐλήμφθην

If the verb stem ends in χ or γ, those letters become χ.

ἄγω → ἤχθην

If the verb stem ends in τ, δ, or θ, those letters drop out and are replaced by σ.

πείθω → ἐπείσθην

2. Aorist Passive Subjunctive

a. The aorist passive subjunctive is formed by finding the aorist passive stem (remove the augment and the ending: ἐλύθην → λυθ-) and adding the same endings as were used to form the present *active* subjunctive:

Aorist Passive Subjunctive

Singular	Plural
λυθῶ	λυθῶμεν
λυθῇς	λυθῆτε
λυθῇ	λυθῶσι(ν)

Note that the accent is a circumflex on the connecting vowel of the ending.

c. There are a few verbs that have a second aorist passive form, i.e., γράφω → ἐγράφην (compare the second aorist and the second perfect). The endings will be the same, but there is no -θ- to distinguish the second aorist passive. These forms must be learned with each verb. (For principal parts, consult the Greek-English vocabulary in the back of this grammar or a lexicon.)

3. Future Passive Tense

a. The future passive tense is formed on the aorist passive stem. Remove the augment (ἐλύθην→λυθην) and then the *ending* (but leave the connecting vowel): λυθη-. To this add a -σ- (the sign of the future) and the regular primary passive endings.

Future Passive Indicative

Singular		Plural
λυθήσομαι	I shall be loosed	λυθησόμεθα
λυθήσῃ	etc.	λυθήσεσθε
λυθήσεται		λυθήσονται

b. If the aorist passive principal part is a second aorist, the same procedure is followed to form the future passive: e.g., ἐγράφην→γραφη- (stem).

Second Future Passive Indicative

Singular		Plural
γραφήσομαι	I shall be written	γραφησόμεθα
γραφήσῃ	etc.	γραφήσεσθε
γραφήσεται		γραφήσονται

4. Future Active Indicative of εἰμί

	Singular		Plural
ἔσομαι	I shall be	ἐσόμεθα	we shall be
ἔσῃ	you will be	ἔσεσθε	you (pl.) will be
ἔσται	he, she, it will be	ἔσονται	they will be

Vocabulary

Verbs:

βαστάζω	bear, carry
γνωρίζω	make known
ὑπακούω	obey (with genitive)

Nouns:

ὁ ἄνεμος	wind
ἡ διαθήκη	covenant
ἡ διακονία	service, ministry
ἡ ἑορτή	feast
ἡ θυσία	sacrifice
ἡ μετάνοια	repentance
ἡ ὀργή	wrath, anger
ἡ προσευχή	prayer
ἡ ὑπομονή	steadfast endurance

Adjective:

ἐκλεκτός, -η, -ον	elect, chosen
περισσός, -η, -ον	abundant, excessive
πτωχός, -η, -ον	poor

Preposition:

ἀντί	instead of (with genitive)

Exercises

A. Translate into English:

1. ταῦτα ἐγράφη ἐν ταῖς γράφαις;
2. ἐλήμφθησαν εἰς τὸ ἱερὸν πειρασθῆναι ὑπὸ τοῦ κακοῦ.
3. Ἰησοῦς ἐγερθήσεται ἐν δόξῃ ἵνα οἱ νεκροὶ ἐγερθῶσιν ἀπὸ τῆς ὁδοῦ ἁμαρτίας.

4. ἡ ὀργὴ τοῦ θεοῦ ἑτοιμασθήσεται ἐκείνοις ἐὰν μὴ σωθῶσιν ὑπὸ τοῦ κυρίου τῆς ἀγάπης.

5. ἡ ὑπομονὴ τῆς προσευχῆς δικαίου ἤχθη ὑπὸ τοῦ κυρίου ἀπὸ τῆς ἐρήμου εἰς τὴν βασιλείαν διακονίας.

6. αἱ προσευχαὶ πτωχοῦ ἀκουσθήσονται ἵνα οὗτοι γένωνται υἱοὶ τοῦ θεοῦ τῆς ἀγάπης.

7. ἡ διακονία τῆς διαθήκης γνωρίζει τοῖς ἐκλεκτοῖς τὴν περισσὴν ἀγάπην τῆς βασιλείας.

B. Translate into Greek:

1. The prayers of a poor man will be raised toward the throne of God.

2. Were you taught by the wisdom of those men?

3. The kingdom of God will be proclaimed by the good people of this world.

4. These things will be written in the law of God.

5. The words of the master were heard by the people in order that the covenant might be believed by the evil slaves.

LESSON XVI

1. Third Declension Nouns

a. The third declension contains the remainder of Greek nouns not included in the first and second declensions. This causes some difficulty in learning to decline the many varieties of nouns which fall under this general category. Since there are numerous nouns in this grouping, one must learn not only the nominative singular form but the genitive singular form also, since this is the form from which the noun stem is derived. The stem is determined by the removal of the -ος from the genitive singular form.

νύξ, νυκτός (night): stem = νυκτ-

Once the noun stem is determined, the following endings are usually used in third declension nouns:

	Singular		**Plural**	
	Masc. and Fem.	**Neuter**	**Masc. and Fem.**	**Neuter**
Nom.	-ς or none	none	-ες	-α
Gen.	-ος	-ος	-ων	-ων
Dat.	-ι	-ι	-σι(ν)	-σι(ν)
Acc.	-ν or -α	none	-ας	-α
Voc.	none, or same as nominative or same as stem		-ες	-α

Note that the masculine and feminine endings are identical in third declension nouns. The definite article must be learned with each third declension noun for gender, so that proper adjectival forms may be used when needed.

b. *"Regular" Third Declension*

i. ἡ νύξ, τῆς νυκτός (night)

	Singular	**Plural**
Nom.	ἡ νύξ	αἱ νύκτες
Gen.	τῆς νυκτός	τῶν νυκτῶν
Dat.	τῇ νυκτί	ταῖς νυξί
Acc.	τὴν νύκτα	τὰς νύκτας

ii. ὁ ἄρχων, τοῦ ἄρχοντος (ruler, prince)

Nom.	ὁ ἄρχων	οἱ ἄρχοντες
Gen.	τοῦ ἄρχοντος	τῶν ἀρχόντων
Dat.	τῷ ἄρχοντι	τοῖς ἄρχουσι(ν)
Acc.	τὸν ἄρχοντα	τοὺς ἄρχοντας

2. Peculiarities of Third Declension Forms

a. If the nominative singular and the dative plural seem confusing to the student, one is reminded of the rules for combinations of consonants with σ. For example, if the basic stem is νυκτ-, add in the nominative singular σ: τ drops before σ→νυκσ; κ + σ = ξ—νύξ. The same process yields νυξί in the dative plural!

b. In the noun ἄρχων (stem: ἀρχοντ-), a similar pattern exists: τ drops before σ→ἀρχονσι. But the Greeks did not like the nu before a sigma, and this too drops out. The remaining vowel (in this case ο) is compensatorily lengthened for the omission of the ν—ἄρχουσι.

3. Four "Types" of Third Declension Nouns

a. The preceding is the usual way for a third declension noun to be declined. Each noun, however, has its own peculiarities which must be observed. If the basic guidelines are followed (i.e., genitive singular, and endings), there will be little difficulty recognizing third declension forms.

b. In addition to "regular" third declension nouns there are four basic "types" of third declension nouns with which the student should be familiar, each of which has its own peculiarities (see the vocabulary list below): (i) neuter nouns of the ὄνομα type, (ii) feminine nouns (usually abstract of the πόλις type), (iii) masculine nouns of the βασιλεύς type, (iv) neuter nouns of the γένος type.

i. τὸ ὄνομα (stem: ονοματ-)

Nom.	τὸ ὄνομα	τὰ	ὀνόματα
Gen.	τοῦ ὀνόματος	τῶν	ὀνομάτων
Dat.	τῷ ὀνόματι	τοῖς	ὀνόμασι(ν)
Acc.	τὸ ὄνομα	τὰ	ὀνόματα

ii. ἡ πόλις (stem: πολι-)

Nom.	ἡ πόλις	αἱ	πόλεις
Gen.	τῆς πόλεως	τῶν	πόλεων
Dat.	τῇ πόλει	ταῖς	πόλεσι(ν)
Acc.	τὴν πόλιν	τὰς	πόλεις

Note the accent in the genitive singular and plural for the πόλις type.

iii. ὁ βασιλεύς (stem: βασιλευ-)

Nom.	ὁ βασιλεύς	οἱ	βασιλεῖς
Gen.	τοῦ βασιλέως	τῶν	βασιλέων
Dat.	τῷ βασιλεῖ	τοῖς	βασιλεῦσι(ν)
Acc.	τὸν βασιλέα	τοὺς	βασιλεῖς

iv. τὸ γένος (stem: γενεσ-)

Nom.	τὸ γένος	τὰ γένη
Gen.	τοῦ γένους	τῶν γενῶν
Dat.	τῷ γένει	τοῖς γένεσι(ν)
Acc.	τὸ γένος	τὰ γένη

c. In dealing with third declension nouns these points must be kept in mind: (1) the basic endings, (2) the genitive singular for the stem, (3) the fact that there are many variations.

Vocabulary

Nouns:

τὸ αἷμα, τοῦ αἵματος	blood
τὸ γράμμα, τοῦ γράμματος	letter
τὸ θέλημα, τοῦ θελήματος	will
τὸ ὄνομα, τοῦ ὀνόματος	name
τὸ πνεῦμα, τοῦ πνεύματος	spirit, wind
τὸ χάρισμα, τοῦ χαρίσματος	free gift
ἡ ἀνάστασις, τῆς ἀναστάσεως	resurrection
ἡ γνῶσις, τῆς γνώσεως	knowledge
ἡ δύναμις, τῆς δυνάμεως	power
ἡ κρίσις, τῆς κρίσεως	judgment
ἡ πόλις, τῆς πόλεως	city
ὁ ἀρχιερεύς, τοῦ ἀρχιερέως	chief priest
ὁ βασιλεύς, τοῦ βασιλέως	king
ὁ γραμματεύς, τοῦ γραμματέως	scribe
ὁ ἱερεύς, τοῦ ἱερέως	priest
τὸ γένος, τοῦ γένους	race
τὸ ἔθνος, τοῦ ἔθνους	nation
τὸ ἔλεος, τοῦ ἐλέους	mercy

τὸ ἔτος, τοῦ ἔτους   year
τὸ μέρος, τοῦ μέρους   part
τὸ πλῆθος, τοῦ πλήθους   crowd, multitude
τὸ τέλος, τοῦ τέλους   end, goal

Preposition:
διά   through (with genitive);
       because of (with accusative)

Exercises

A.   Translate into English:

1.   τὸ αἷμα τῆς ἀναστάσεως ἐκηρύχθη ἐν τῇ πόλει τοῦ βασιλέως τῶν ἐθνῶν.

2.   ἀγώμεθα ὑπὸ τῆς δυνάμεως τοῦ ἀγαθοῦ ὀνόματος ἵνα μένωμεν ἐν τῇ πόλει τῆς γνώσεως.

3.   οἱ ἱερεῖς οὗτοι ἐγερθήσονται ὑπὸ τοῦ ἁγίου πνεύματος ἐν τῷ ὀνόματι τοῦ Ἰησοῦ.

4.   ἡ δικαιοσύνη τοῦ θεοῦ ἔσωσεν τὸ πλῆθος ἐκ τῶν κακῶν δυνάμεων, τὸ δὲ χάρισμα τοῦ υἱοῦ αὐτοῦ μένει διὰ τῆς νυκτός.

5.   οὗτος ὁ ἄρχων ἐδίωξεν τοὺς μαθητὰς τοῦ κυρίου, τὸ δὲ θέλημα τοῦ γραμματέως κατέλυσεν τὰ ἔτη τοῦ ἐλέους ἐν τῇ φυλακῇ τοῦ κακοῦ πνεύματος.

6.   τὸ αἷμα τῶν ἁγίων ἐκαθάριζεν τὰς ἁμαρτίας τῶν ἱερέων ἵνα τὰ ἔθνη λαμβάνῃ ἔλεος ἐν τῇ κρίσει.

7.   εἰ ὁ βασιλεὺς ἦλθεν εἰς τὴν πόλιν, τὸ πνεῦμα καὶ τὸ χάρισμα οὐκ ὑπήχθη εἰς τὴν κρίσιν.

B. Translate into Greek:

1. The name of the ruler will be written in the hearts of the scribes in order that the resurrection may come in power.
2. This spirit has looked into the hearts of the priests in order that the year of mercy may come.
3. The good kings of the world are hearing the sounds of mercy at the time of the end.

LESSON XVII

1. Participles (Present, Active-Middle-Passive)

a. In order to *know* the Greek language one must understand the Greek verbal system, especially participles. A participle is a *verbal adjective,* and, therefore, it has characteristics of both verbs and adjectives. As a verb, it has tense, voice, and complements (such as objects); as an adjective, it has gender, number, and case (therefore, it must agree with the noun or pronoun it modifies in gender, number, and case). A participle is a verb form, built on a verb stem, but declined as an adjective.

b. *Declension of the Present Active Participle of* εἰμί

Singular

	Masculine	Feminine	Neuter
Nom.	ὤν	οὖσα	ὄν
Gen.	ὄντος	οὔσης	ὄντος
Dat.	ὄντι	οὔσῃ	ὄντι
Acc.	ὄντα	οὖσαν	ὄν

Plural

	Masculine	Feminine	Neuter
Nom.	ὄντες	οὖσαι	ὄντα
Gen.	ὄντων	οὐσῶν	ὄντων
Dat.	οὖσι(ν)	οὔσαις	οὖσι(ν)
Acc.	ὄντας	οὔσας	ὄντα

This must be mastered.

86

Note that the masculine and neuter are declined as third declension nouns, and the feminine follows the first declension δόξα type.

c. To form the *present active participle* of a verb, first find the present stem (λύω→λυ-). To this stem add *as endings* the same forms learned as the present participle of εἰμί:

Singular

	Masculine	**Feminine**	**Neuter**
Nom.	λύων	λύουσα	λῦον
Gen.	λύοντος	λυούσης	λύοντος
Dat.	λύοντι	λυούσῃ	λύοντι
Acc.	λύοντα	λύουσαν	λῦον

Plural

Nom.	λύοντες	λύουσαι	λύοντα
Gen.	λυόντων	λυουσῶν	λυόντων
Dat.	λύουσι(ν)	λυούσαις	λύουσι(ν)
Acc.	λύοντας	λυούσας	λύοντα

The accent on the participle is not recessive. Insofar as possible (review the rules for noun accentuation) the accent remains where it was on the present tense principal part (λύω→λύων, λύοντος, etc.). Thus, the rule is the same as that for nouns and adjectives. The accent on the genitive feminine plural becomes a circumflex on the ultima, as in the first declension.

d. To form the present middle or passive participle of a verb, find the present stem (λυ-), and to this add as a suffix -ομεν (λυομεν) and the regular endings of the first and second declension adjectives!

Singular

	Masculine	Feminine	Neuter
Nom.	λυόμενος	λυομένη	λυόμενον
Gen.	λυομένου	λυομένης	λυομένου
Dat.	λυομένῳ	λυομένῃ	λυομένῳ
Acc.	λυόμενον	λυομένην	λυόμενον

Plural

Nom.	λυόμενοι	λυόμεναι	λυόμενα
Gen.	λυομένων	λυομένων	λυομένων
Dat.	λυομένοις	λυομέναις	λυομένοις
Acc.	λυομένους	λυομένας	λυόμενα

2. Translation of Participles

a. The present participle is generally translated by the English present participle, but there is no *single* way to translate the participle. It may remain a participle in translation (e.g., having, being, running), or the translator may wish to make a finite clause to convey the meaning.

> ὁ λύων βασιλεύς
> the loosing king *or* the king who is loosing

b. The participle usually has no time of its own. The chief function of the tense is *kind of action*. The "time" of a participle is, therefore, determined by its relationship with the main verb.

> i. The "time" of the present participle is usually considered to be simultaneous with the action of the main verb, be that action present, past, or future: "the one who is loosing" (with present); "the one who was loosing" (with past); or "the one who is about to (*or* going to) loose" (with future).

    ii. Because the aorist indicates undefined action, the "time" of the aorist participle usually indicates action *prior to* the action of the main verb, be that past, present, or future: "the man who loosed" (with present); "the man who had loosed" (with past); "or "the man who looses" (with future). (For the aorist participle, see Lesson XVIII).

    iii. In each instance, the context is determinative.

3. Positions of the Participle

    a. The participle may immediately follow the definite article; that is, it may be in the attributive position (compare the adjective). When found in this setting, a participle is translated in much the same way as an attributive adjective.

    ὁ λέγων μαθητής
        the speaking disciple *or* the disciple, the one who is speaking
    or the disciple who is speaking

As with the adjective, the participle may stand alone with the article.

    ὁ λέγων the one who is speaking

    b. A participle may be used in the predicative position, that is, *not* immediately following the definite article. This use of the participle usually results in a *circumstantial* (adverbial) *clause* introduced by "while" for a present participle ("after" or "when" for an aorist participle).

    λέγων ὁ μαθητής while speaking the disciple

4. Genitive Absolute Construction

    The genitive absolute is a special construction with the predicative participle. This construction forms a circumstantial clause (i.e., "while," "after," "when"), but the primary factor here is that the noun in the clause does not have a syntactical relationship with any other part of the sentence. That is, it is not the subject, object, etc., in the main clause. Therefore, to form such a construction in Greek both the noun (or pronoun) and the participle are placed in the genitive case and when translated form a separate circumstantial clause.

> τοῦ βασιλέως ἐρχομένου ὁ μαθητὴς εἶπεν τῷ ὄχλῳ.
> While the king was coming, the disciple spoke to the crowd.

Note that the noun "king" has no syntactical relationship with the main clause. Therefore, it and the participle are in the genitive case. Usually a genitive absolute construction is found at the beginning of a sentence or the clause with which it is connected.

Vocabulary

Nouns:

ὁ αἰών, τοῦ αἰῶνος	age, world
ὁ ἀμπελών, τοῦ ἀμπελῶνος	vineyard
ἡ ἄφεσις, τῆς ἀφέσεως	forgiveness
ἡ ἐλπίς, τῆς ἐλπίδος	hope
τὸ εὐαγγέλιον	good news
ἡ κτίσις, τῆς κτίσεως	creation
ὁ πούς, τοῦ ποδός	foot
τὸ ῥῆμα, τοῦ ῥήματος	word
ἡ σάρξ, τῆς σαρκός	flesh
τὸ σπέρμα, τοῦ σπέρματος	seed
τὸ στόμα, τοῦ στόματος	mouth
τὸ σῶμα, τοῦ σώματος	body
τὸ φῶς, τοῦ φωτός	light
ἡ χάρις, τῆς χάριτος	grace
ἡ σκοτία	darkness

Exercises

A. Translate into English:

1. οἱ προφῆται τοῦ κακοῦ ἦλθον εἰς τὴν ἔρημον τῶν βασιλέων διωκομένων ὑπὸ τοῦ υἱοῦ αὐτοῦ.

2. οἱ σωζόμενοι ὑπὸ τοῦ ἄρχοντος τῆς σκοτίας καταλυθήσονται ἐν ἐκείναις ταῖς ἐσχάταις ἡμέραις.

3. εἰ οἱ ὑπακούοντες τοῦ κυρίου προσεύχοντο, ἂν τὰ τέκνα τοῦ κακοῦ ἤρχετο εἰς τὸν οἶκον δικαιοσύνης.

4. ἐὰν σώσητε τὴν σάρκα τοῦ σώματος, τὰ φῶτα τῆς ἐλπίδος πιστευθήσεται ὑπὸ τῶν ἀρχόντων διδασκόντων ἐν τῷ ἀμπελῶνε.

5. αὐτῶν ἀγόντων τὰ σώματα τῶν κακῶν εἰς τὸν ἀμπελῶνα οἱ ἀποκτείνοντες τοὺς ἁγίους ἐγνώριζον τὴν ὀργὴν αὐτῶν.

6. εἶδον τοὺς μένοντας ἐν τῷ ἱερῷ ἵνα διδάσκοντες τὰ τέκνα τοῦ πνεύματος κηρύξωσιν τὸ εὐαγγέλιον τὸ σῶζον τούτους.

7. πιστεύοντες ἐν τῷ ὀνόματι τοῦ Ἰησοῦ γινώμεθα οἱ κηρύσσοντες τὴν βασιλείαν τοῦ θεοῦ.

B. Translate into Greek:

1. The ones who are loosing the sons of the truth are sending the ones teaching wisdom into the age of faith.

2. While the words were being spoken in the temple, these good people received the ones who were pursuing the truth of God.

3. While hearing the words of the priest, the prophets of the spirit are saluting the days of righteousness.

1. Aorist Active and Middle Participles

a. The first aorist active participle is formed by finding the aorist stem (e.g., ἔλυσα), removing the ending and the augment (λυσ), and adding the following endings:

Singular

	Masculine	**Feminine**	**Neuter**
Nom.	-ας	-ασα	-αν
Gen.	-αντος	-ασης	-αντος
Dat.	-αντι	-αση	-αντι
Acc.	-αντα	-ασαν	-αν

Plural

	Masculine	**Feminine**	**Neuter**
Nom.	-αντες	-ασαι	-αντα
Gen.	-αντων	-ασων	-αντων
Dat.	-ασι(ν)	-ασαις	-ασι(ν)
Acc.	-αντας	-ασας	-αντα

Singular

	Masculine	**Feminine**	**Neuter**
Nom.	λύσας	λύσασα	λῦσαν
Gen.	λύσαντος	λυσάσης	λύσαντος
Dat.	λύσαντι	λυσάσῃ	λύσαντι
Acc.	λύσαντα	λύσασαν	λῦσαν

Plural

Nom.	λύσαντες	λύσασαι	λύσαντα
Gen.	λυσάντων	λυσασῶν	λυσάντων
Dat.	λύσασι(ν)	λυσάσαις	λύσασι(ν)
Acc.	λύσαντας	λυσάσας	λύσαντα

b. The first aorist middle participle is formed by taking the aorist stem (λυσ-) and adding a connecting vowel -α- and the familiar middle/passive participle ending -μενος, -η, -ον.

Singular

	Masculine	Feminine	Neuter
Nom.	λυσάμενος	λυσαμένη	λυσάμενον
Gen.	λυσαμένου	λυσαμένης	λυσαμένου
Dat.	λυσαμένῳ	λυσαμένῃ	λυσαμένῳ
Acc.	λυσάμενον	λυσαμένην	λυσάμενον

Plural

Nom.	λυσάμενοι	λυσάμεναι	λυσάμενα
Gen.	λυσαμένων	λυσαμένων	λυσαμένων
Dat.	λυσαμένοις	λυσαμέναις	λυσαμένοις
Acc.	λυσαμένους	λυσαμένας	λυσάμενα

This participle is declined like the adjective ἀγαθός, -η, -ον except for the accent.

c. The second aorist active participle is formed by finding the aorist stem (e.g., εἶδον), removing the ending and the augment (ιδ-), and adding the same endings that were added to the *present* active participle.

Singular

	Masculine	**Feminine**	**Neuter**
Nom.	ἰδών	ἰδοῦσα	ἰδόν
Gen.	ἰδόντος	ἰδούσης	ἰδόντος
Dat.	ἰδόντι	ἰδούσῃ	ἰδόντι
Acc.	ἰδόντα	ἰδοῦσαν	ἰδόν

Plural

Nom.	ἰδόντες	ἰδοῦσαι	ἰδόντα
Gen.	ἰδόντων	ἰδουσῶν	ἰδόντων
Dat.	ἰδοῦσι(ν)	ἰδούσαις	ἰδοῦσι(ν)
Acc.	ἰδόντας	ἰδούσας	ἰδόντα

d. The second aorist middle participle is formed by finding the stem (ἰδ-) and adding the same endings as the present middle/passive participle: -ομενος, -η, -ον.

Singular

	Masculine	**Feminine**	**Neuter**
Nom.	ἰδόμενος	ἰδομένη	ἰδόμενον
Gen.	ἰδομένου	ἰδομένης	ἰδομένου
Dat.	ἰδομένῳ	ἰδομένῃ	ἰδομένῳ
Acc.	ἰδόμενον	ἰδομένην	ἰδόμενον

Plural

Nom.	ἰδόμενοι	ἰδόμεναι	ἰδόμενα
Gen.	ἰδομένων	ἰδομένων	ἰδομένων
Dat.	ἰδομένοις	ἰδομέναις	ἰδομένοις
Acc.	ἰδομένους	ἰδομένας	ἰδόμενα

It also is declined like the adjective ἀγαθός, -η, -ον, except for the accent.

2. Aorist Passive Participle

The aorist passive participle is built on the aorist passive stem (ἐλύθην→λυθ-). To this the following endings are added:

Singular

	Masculine	Feminine	Neuter
Nom.	-εις	-εισα	-εν
Gen.	-εντος	-εισης	-εντος
Dat.	-εντι	-εισῃ	-εντι
Acc.	-εντα	-εισαν	-εν

Plural

	Masculine	Feminine	Neuter
Nom.	-εντες	-εισαι	-εντα
Gen.	-εντων	-εισων	-εντων
Dat.	-εισι(ν)	-εισαις	-εισι(ν)
Acc.	-εντας	-εισας	-εντα

Singular

Nom.	λυθείς	λυθεῖσα	λυθέν
Gen.	λυθέντος	λυθείσης	λυθέντος
Dat.	λυθέντι	λυθείσῃ	λυθέντι
Acc.	λυθέντα	λυθεῖσαν	λυθέν

Plural

Nom.	λυθέντες	λυθεῖσαι	λυθέντα
Gen.	λυθέντων	λυθεισῶν	λυθέντων
Dat.	λυθεῖσι(ν)	λυθείσαις	λυθεῖσι(ν)
Acc.	λυθέντας	λυθείσας	λυθέντα

Note that the accentuation pattern for the aorist passive participle is the same as that of the second aorist active participle.

Vocabulary

Verbs:

πορεύομαι	go, proceed
ὑπάρχω	be, exist

Nouns:

ὁ ἀνήρ, τοῦ ἀνδρός	man, husband
ἡ γυνή, τῆς γυναικός	woman, wife
ἡ θλῖψις, τῆς θλίψεως	tribulation
ἡ θυγάτηρ, τῆς θυγατρός	daughter
ἡ θύρα	door
ἡ μήτηρ, τῆς μητρός	mother
ὁ πατήρ, τοῦ πατρός	father
ἡ πίστις, τῆς πίστεως	faith, trust
τὸ σκότος, τοῦ σκότους	darkness
ἡ συνείδησις, τῆς συνειδήσεως	conscience
τὸ ὕδωρ, τοῦ ὕδατος	water

Adverb:

σήμερον	today

Preposition:

χωρίς	apart from, without (with genitive)

Exercises

A. Translate into English:

1. πίστει σωζόμεθα ὅτι οἱ ὄντες δίκαιοι ἐκήρυξαν τὸ εὐαγγέλιον τὸ δίδαξαν ἀγάπην καὶ ἀλήθειαν.

2. οἱ ἰδόντες τὴν βασιλείαν τοῦ σκότους ἤχθησαν εἰς τὸ φῶς τοῦ κόσμου ὑπὸ τῶν κηρυσσόντων τὸν λόγον.

3. αὐτῶν πιστευσάντων οἱ πατέρες ἡμῶν ἐπορεύθησαν εἰς τὸ ὕδωρ ἵνα βαπτισθῶμεν ὑπὸ τῶν θυγατέρων ὑμῶν.

4. πεμφθέντος αὐτοῦ ἐκ τοῦ δεχομένου τὰ καλὰ δῶρα αἱ ἐσθίουσαι τοὺς ἄρτους ἤρχοντο ἄγειν τούτους εἰς τὸν οἶκον τῆς μητρός.

5. ἐὰν σήμερον ἄρξωνται πιστεῦσαι, οἱ ἀκούσαντες ἐγερθήσονται ἀπὸ τοῦ κόσμου τοῦ πνεύματος εἰς τὸ ἔθνος τῶν ἐλπισάντων.

6. αὐτῶν ἐλθόντων εἰς θλῖψιν οἱ λύσαντες τὴν συνείδησιν τῆς γυναικὸς ἐπορεύοντο ἀπὸ τῆς ὁδοῦ τῆς εἰρήνης.

7. οἱ ἄγοντες τὸ εὐαγγέλιον ὑπακούσουσιν τοῦ κυρίου τοῦ ἀπολύσαντος τὸν λαὸν ἐκ τοῦ τόπου τοῦ σκότους.

B. Translate into Greek:

1. The ones who are proceeding into the kingdom of darkness will be raised with the ones who have not heard the words of life.

2. After the mothers loosed the children, the husband of the one leading those women released the slaves from the vineyard.

3. Let us continue to proclaim the kingdom of God to those who have not come into the synagogue of the righteous.

Lesson XIX

1. Relative Pronouns

a. The declension of the relative pronouns (who, which) is as follows:

Singular

	Masculine	Feminine	Neuter
Nom.	ὅς	ἥ	ὅ
Gen.	οὗ	ἧς	οὗ
Dat.	ᾧ	ᾗ	ᾧ
Acc.	ὅν	ἥν	ὅ

Plural

	Masculine	Feminine	Neuter
Nom.	οἵ	αἵ	ἅ
Gen.	ὧν	ὧν	ὧν
Dat.	οἷς	αἷς	οἷς
Acc.	οὕς	ἅς	ἅ

Note that the relative pronoun follows the first and second declension endings for αὐτός and ἐκεῖνος, except that here the endings stand alone with a rough breathing and an accent.

b. The relative pronoun must agree in gender and number with its antecedent but usually takes its case from the usage in its own clause.

ὁ δοῦλος ὅν ἔλαβον εἰσῆλθεν εἰς τὸν οἶκον.
The slave whom I received came into the house.

Gender and number: masculine singular, to agree with the antecedent, "slave."

Case: accusative, because it is the direct object of the verb "receive" in its clause.

There are a few instances when the relative pronoun is "attracted" to the case of the antecedent. This phenomenon usually takes place (1) when the antecedent is in the genitive (or less frequently the dative) case, (2) when the pronoun would be in the accusative in its own clause, and (3) usually when the two words are immediately juxtaposed to each other.

ὑπήκουσα τοῦ λόγου οὗ εἶπές μοι.

I obeyed the word which you spoke to me.

2. Interrogative Pronouns

a. The declension of the interrogative pronoun (who?, which?, what?) is as follows:

Singular

	Masc. and Fem.	Neuter
Nom.	τίς	τί
Gen.	τίνος	τίνος
Dat.	τίνι	τίνι
Acc.	τίνα	τί

Plural

	Masc. and Fem.	Neuter
Nom.	τίνες	τίνα
Gen.	τίνων	τίνων
Dat.	τίσι(ν)	τίσι(ν)
Acc.	τίνας	τίνα

b. The interrogative pronoun is declined according to the third declension pattern. Note that the masculine and feminine forms are identical.

c. The interrogative pronoun has an acute accent which is *never* changed to a grave.

> τίς λέγει;
> Who is speaking?
> τίνας εἶδον;
> Whom did they see?
> τίνες ἄνθρωποι εἰσῆλθον εἰς τὸν οἶκον;
> Which men came into the house?

d. The neuter singular τί may be used adverbially as "why?"

> τί λέγουσιν ταῦτα;
> Why are they saying these things?

3. Indefinite Pronouns

a. The declension of the indefinite pronoun (any, some) is as follows:

Singular

	Masc. and Fem.	Neuter
Nom.	τὶς	τὶ
Gen.	τινός	τινός
Dat.	τινί	τινί
Acc.	τινά	τὶ

Plural

	Masc. and Fem.	**Neuter**
Nom.	τίνές	τινά
Gen.	τινῶν	τινῶν
Dat.	τισί(ν)	τισί(ν)
Acc.	τινάς	τινά

Note that the spelling of the indefinite pronoun is identical to the interrogative pronoun. The difference is that the indefinite pronoun is enclitic (see Lesson VIII 3).

b. The indefinite is usually translated "one," "a certain one," "some one," "some," or "some ones (people)."

> τὶς ἦλθεν εἰς τὸ ἱερόν
> A certain man went into the temple.

Vocabulary

Verbs:

ξηραίνω	dry up
χορτάζω	eat to the full, be satisfied

Nouns:

τὸ βάπτισμα, τοῦ βαπτίσματος	baptism
τὸ βρῶμα, τοῦ βρώματος	food
ὁ γονεύς, τοῦ γονέως	parent
ἡ εὐλογία	blessing
ἡ εὐσέβεια	piety, godliness
ὁ λῃστής	robber
ἡ ῥίζα	root
ἡ σφραγίς, τῆς σφραγῖδος	seal

Preposition:

ἐπί	upon (with dative)

Exercises

A.   Translate into English:

1.   ὃ γέγραφα γέγραφα.
2.   τί πεπίστευκας ἐν τῷ λόγῳ τῷ γραφομένῳ ἐπὶ τῇ σφραγῖδι;
3.   τὸ βρῶμα ὃ ἐγὼ ἔφαγον ἦν ζωὴ καὶ ἀλήθεια.
4.   τινὲς οὐ πιστεύουσιν ὅτι οὗτοι γέγοναν τέκνα τοῦ κακοῦ τοῦ ἄγοντός τινας εἰς ἁμαρτίαν.
5.   ἡ ῥίζα ξηραίνει ἵνα οἱ λῃσταὶ μὴ χορτάζωσιν βρώματι.
6.   ἡ εὐλογία τῆς εὐσεβείας ἡ λυθεῖσα ἐν ταῖς καρδίαις τῶν ἀνδρῶν ἄξει λῃστὰς εἰς τὴν θλῖψιν.
7.   τὸ ποτήριον ὃ ἐγὼ κατέφαγον ἄξει τινὰς εἰς τὴν βασιλείαν τοῦ θεοῦ.
8.   ἡ σφραγὶς τῆς εὐλογίας ἧς ἐλάβετε ἀπό μου γέγραπται ἐν τῷ βιβλίῳ τῆς ζωῆς.

B.   Translate into Greek:

1.   The baptism with which I am going to be baptized will save men from their sins.
2.   The blessing of the lord was sent by his messenger whom those men killed because he proclaimed the godliness of the world.
3.   Why have you come into the place which was not seen by our teachers?

Lesson XX

1. Declension and Uses of πᾶς

a. *Declension*

Singular

	Masculine	Feminine	Neuter
Nom.	πᾶς	πᾶσα	πᾶν
Gen.	παντός	πάσης	παντός
Dat.	παντί	πάσῃ	παντί
Acc.	πάντα	πᾶσαν	πᾶν

Plural

	Masculine	Feminine	Neuter
Nom.	πάντες	πᾶσαι	πάντα
Gen.	πάντων	πασῶν	πάντων
Dat.	πᾶσι(ν)	πάσαις	πᾶσι(ν)
Acc.	πάντας	πάσας	πάντα

Note the similarity of the endings for πᾶς to the endings of the aorist active participle.

b. πᾶς is generally translated "every" in the singular, "all" in the plural. There are, however, certain nuances that must be kept in mind.

       i. πᾶς may be used in the attributive position to indicate entirety. This may mean "all" in the sense of each and every, or it may indicate the totality of a given group or set of people or

103

things. Thus, it may be translated "whole" or "entire."

ὁ πᾶς θερισμός   the entire harvest

ii. πᾶς may be used in the predicative position and then usually means "all" in the sense of most, many, a large number (but not necessarily indicating totality).

πᾶς ὁ θερισμός   all the harvest, most of the harvest

iii. πᾶς may be used with a noun not having a definite article and usually means "every."

πᾶς θερισμός   every harvest

iv. πᾶς plus the article may be used with a participle.

πᾶς ὁ εὐφραίνων   everyone who is rejoicing
πάντες οἱ εὐφραίνοντες all who are rejoicing

2. Adjectives of the Third Declension

a. Most adjectives in Greek are declined according to the first and second declension paradigm (compare ἀγαθός). There are, however, approximately sixty adjectives that follow the paradigm of the third declension. The stem for third declension adjectives is -ες (e.g., ἀληθες), and these adjectives may be easily identified from the vocabulary lists since they are designated as ἀληθής, ἀληθές.

b. There is a great degree of similarity between this declension of adjectives and the γένος "type" of third declension nouns.

	Singular Masc. and Fem.	Neuter
Nom.	ἀληθής	ἀληθές
Gen.	ἀληθοῦς	ἀληθοῦς
Dat.	ἀληθεῖ	ἀληθεῖ
Acc.	ἀληθῆ ₑ	ἀληθές

	Plural	
Nom.	ἀληθεῖς	ἀληθῆ ˎ
Gen.	ἀληθῶν	ἀληθῶν
Dat.	ἀληθέσι(ν)	ἀληθέσι(ν)
Acc.	ἀληθεῖς	ἀληθῆ ˎ

c. All the general rules governing adjectives apply to third declension adjectives—attributive and predicative positions, agreement with nouns in gender, number, and case.

3. Mixed Adjectives

There are some "mixed" adjectives in Greek; that is, adjectives that have some forms that follow the first and second declension paradigm (ἀγαθός) and some forms that follow the third declension. Two such adjectives are πολύς (much) and μέγας (great). It is immediately evident by examining the paradigms that the nominative and accusative singulars of the masculine and neuter follow the third declension. The remaining forms of both (each with its own peculiarities) follow the first and second declension patterns.

a. Declension of πολύς

Singular

	Masculine	Feminine	Neuter
Nom.	πολύς ⌐	πολλή	πολύ ⌐
Gen.	πολλοῦ	πολλῆς	πολλοῦ
Dat.	πολλῷ	πολλῇ	πολλῷ
Acc.	πολύν ⌐	πολλήν	πολύ ⌐

Plural

	Masculine	Feminine	Neuter
Nom.	πολλοί	πολλαί	πολλά
Gen.	πολλῶν	πολλῶν	πολλῶν
Dat.	πολλοῖς	πολλαῖς	πολλοῖς
Acc.	πολλούς	πολλάς	πολλά

b. Declension of μέγας

Singular

	Masculine	Feminine	Neuter
Nom	μέγας ⌐	μεγάλη	μέγα ⌐
Gen.	μεγάλου	μεγάλης	μεγάλου
Dat.	μεγάλῳ	μεγάλη	μεγάλῳ
Acc.	μέγαν ⌐	μεγάλην	μέγα ⌐

Plural

	Masculine	Feminine	Neuter
Nom.	μεγάλοι	μεγάλαι	μεγάλα
Gen.	μεγάλων	μεγάλων	μεγάλων
Dat.	μεγάλοις	μεγάλαις	μεγάλοις
Acc.	μεγάλους	μεγάλας	μεγάλα

Vocabulary

Verbs:

εὐφραίνω	rejoice
θύω	sacrifice, kill
μοιχεύω	commit adultery
στηρίζω	establish

Nouns:

ὁ θερισμός	harvest
ὁ κληρονόμος	heir
ἡ παράδοσις, τῆς παραδόσεως	tradition
ὁ σῖτος	wheat
ἡ χείρ, τῆς χειρός	hand

Adjectives:

ἀληθής, ἀληθές	true
ἀσθενής, ἀσθενές	weak, sick
καινός, -η, -ον	new
κοινός, -η, -ον	common, unclean
μονογενής, μονογενές	only begotten
ξένος, -η, -ον	strange
πᾶς, πᾶσα, πᾶν	all, every
ὑγιής, ὑγιές	whole, healthy

Exercises

A. Translate into English:

1. ὁ ἀληθὴς κληρονόμος εὐφραίνει ὅτι πᾶν πνεῦμα ἐλήλυθεν εἰς τὸν κοινὸν οἶκον.

2. εἰ τὸ πνεῦμα ἐδύνατο δέχεσθαι κρίσιν, ἂν ἡ σὰρξ οὐκ ἦν ἀσθενής.

3. δεῖ θεραπευθῆναι ἵνα οὗτοι εἴπωσιν τῇ γυναικὶ τὰ ῥήματα τοῦ μεγάλου βασιλέως.

4. πολλὰ κηρυχθήσεται ὅτι ἡ πίστις πάντων ἔσται μεγάλη.

5. τὰ διδασκόμενα ὑπὸ τοῦ ἀσθενοῦς ἀδελφοῦ ἐθύθη ἵνα ἡ παράδοσις πᾶσα τῶν ἔθνων σωθῇ.

6. πάντων τῶν βασιλέων ἰδόντων τὸν ξένον μεγάλα ἠκούσθη ὑπὸ τοῦ μονογενοῦς υἱοῦ τῆς δόξης.

7. πάντες οἱ κληρονόμοι ἀπεκτείνοντο ἵνα ὁ ἀσθενὴς στηρίζηται χωρὶς τῆς παραδόσεως τοῦ κυρίου.

8. πᾶσαι αἱ μεγάλαι πόλεις τοῦ κόσμου μοιχεύουσιν σὺν τοῖς θερισμοῖς κακοῦ.

B.   Translate into Greek:

1. The great kings of the world will be raised in order that many weak nations may be brought into the tradition of the great city.

2. The healthy man does not wish to be sacrificed because he is not sick.

3. The only-begotten son of glory entered into the temple in order that the weak people of the world may be saved.

LESSON XXI

1. Uses of the Infinitive

There are numerous ways in which the Greek language uses the infinitive.

a. The infinitive is used to complement certain verbs.

ἄξιός ἐστιν λαμβάνειν δόξαν.
She is worthy to receive glory.

b. As in English, the Greek infinitive may be used as a substitute for a (neuter) noun. This is roughly equivalent to the English gerund. When the infinitive is used in this manner, it will sometimes have the neuter definite article (but not always).

τὸ λαμβάνειν τὸ δῶρον πέμψει αὐτοὺς εἰς τὸ ἱερόν.
To receive the gift will send them into the temple.
Or: Receiving the gift will send them into the temple.

c. The infinitive is also used to form certain dependent clauses. When this construction occurs, the infinitive will be found (sometimes with an article) along with a noun or pronoun in the accusative case. (This is called the accusative of general reference.) When this type of construction is translated into English, the noun or pronoun in the accusative case becomes the subject of the dependent clause in English. There are several types of *articular infinitive* clauses. This is the technical term for such constructions even when the article is not present.

    i. The infinitive and its noun/pronoun may follow a preposition.

    πρὸ τοῦ εἰπεῖν τὸν βασιλέα . . .
    Before the king spoke . . .
    Or: Before the king's speaking . . .

The article is in the genitive case because the preposition takes the genitive as the case of its object.

    ii. There are two specialized constructions with the articular infinitive used to express purpose:

        (1) τοῦ + infinitive
        (2) εἰς τὸ . . . + infinitive

These are translated exactly like the ἵνα clause, and there seems to be no real difference of nuance among the three constructions, only a stylistic preference on the part of the writer.

λαμβάνομεν αὐτοὺς τοῦ τὸν ἄνδρα σωθῆναι.
We are receiving them in order that the man may be saved.

ταῦτα εἶπεν εἰς τὸ φαγεῖν αὐτοὺς σὺν τῷ βασιλεῖ.
These things he spoke in order that they might eat with the king.

    iii. The conjunction ὥστε may be used with an infinitive to form a result clause.

εἶπεν τὴν ἀλήθειαν ὥστε τὸν ὄχλον εἰσέρχεσθαι εἰς τὴν ζωήν.
He spoke the truth with the result that the crowd was entering into life.

In certain instances the ὥστε clause may have a finite verb and a subject in the nominative case.

d. In articular infinitive clauses sometimes there is no noun or pronoun in the accusative case. In such instances it is assumed that the subject of the dependent clause is the same as the subject of the main clause of the sentence.

πρὸ τοῦ εἰπεῖν πρὸς τὸν λαὸν οἱ ἀγαθοὶ διδάσκαλοι ἦλθον εἰς τὸν οἶκον.
Before they had spoken to the people, the good teachers came into the house.

e. As with the translation of the participle, generally speaking the "time" of the present infinitive will be simultaneous with the action of the main verb, and the time of the aorist infinitive will be prior to the action of the main verb.

2. Indirect Discourse

a. The Greek language developed a means of reporting indirectly what people said, thought, perceived, heard, saw, etc. This is done frequently in English also:

John said, "I am going to town"—direct discourse.
John said that he was going to town—indirect discourse.

This particular construction was frequently used in Greek writing and is found after verbs of seeing, hearing, knowing, thinking, perceiving, etc. There are three ways in which indirect discourse may be expressed in Greek.

  i. By an articular infinitive clause:

λέγω αὐτὸν εἶναι μωρόν.
I say that he is foolish.
εἴδετε τὸν δοῦλον ἀχθῆναι εἰς ἁμαρτίαν.
You saw that the slave had been led into sin.

  ii. By ὅτι (that) plus a finite verb:

ἔλεγον ὅτι ἡ ἀνομία τῶν ὄχλων καταλύεται ὑπὸ τοῦ προφήτου.
They were saying that the lawlessness of the crowds was being destroyed by the prophet.

When this construction is used, the *original tense and mood* of the verb (from the original statement or thought) must be retained.

iii. By a participle with a noun or pronoun in the accusative case:

ἠκούομεν τινα ἐκβάλλοντα δαιμόνια.
We were hearing that someone was casting out demons.

b. When the original statement was a question, the interrogative particle or pronoun is retained along with the verb in its finite state (see [ii] above).

εἶδον τί ἦν ἐν τῷ τόπῳ ἐκείνῳ.
They saw what was in that place.

c. This particular construction is widely found in Greek literature. One must be alert to the possibility of finding one of these forms almost anywhere or anytime! This is especially true when verbs of knowing, seeing, hearing, thinking, perceiving, or the like are used.

Vocabulary

Nouns:

ἡ ἀνομία	lawlessness
τὸ μυστήριον	mystery
τὸ ὄρος, τοῦ ὄρους	mountain

Adjectives:

ἀλλότριος, -α, -ον	strange, another's
ἡμέτερος, -α, -ον	our
ἱκανός, -η, -ον	sufficient, able
μωρός, -α, -ον	foolish
ὑμέτερος, -α, -ον	your

Adverbs:

ἄνωθεν	from above, again
ἐγγύς	near
μακρόθεν	from afar

Conjunctions:
ὅταν   whenever (with subjunctive)
ὅτε   when

Numeral:
πέντε   five (indeclinable)

Exercises

A.   Translate into English:

1.   πρὸ τοῦ ἰδεῖν αὐτοὺς εἰς τὸν οἶκον ὁ βασιλεὺς ἐγίνωσκεν τὸν ἱερέα εἶναι ἐν τῷ ἱερῷ.

2.   ὁ λέγων τὴν ἀλήθειαν ἀκούεσθαι ἐν τῷ κόσμῳ ἄρχεται κηρῦξαι ὅτι ὁ θεός ἐστιν ἀγαθός.

3.   μετὰ τὸ ἐκβληθῆναι τὸν κακὸν ἐκ τοῦ οὐρανοῦ πάντες οἱ ἄγγελοι ἐγίνωσκον τὸ τέλος τῆς ἁμαρτίας ἐλθεῖν ἐγγύς.

4.   ἡ θλῖψις τῆς ζωῆς ἡ λυθεῖσα ὑπὸ τοῦ κυρίου πέμψει τὸ μυστήριον τῆς βασιλείας εἰς τὸ φῶς τοῦ σκότος καταλύεσθαι.

5.   τοῦ λόγου κηρυσσομένου τινὲς ἀπέθανον ὥστε τὸ ἔθνος τοῦ πνεύματος σώζεσθαι.

6.   Ἰησοῦς ἐγίνωσκεν τί ἦν ἐν τῇ καρδίᾳ ἐκείνου.

7.   τί προσευξώμεθα οὐ γινώσκομεν.

B.   Translate into Greek:

1.   The king of the strange kingdom saw that all the people were beginning to come toward our mountain from afar.

2.   Your lawlessness will be sufficient to release the lawlessness of all evil men.

3.   Before the priest brought the woman into the synagogue, the mystery of the kingdom had been known by all those who were led by the lord.

LESSON XXII

1. Contract Verbs

a. Verbs listed in the lexicon or the vocabulary lists whose stems (the form left after the removal of the first person ending, -ω or -ομαι) end in -α-, -ε-, or -ο- are contract verbs. There is an aversion in Greek to having several short vowels standing alongside each other (compare the augment), and therefore the α, ε, or ο of the verb stem will "contract" with the connecting vowel of the ending. This contraction occurs *only* in the present tense forms, that is, all forms built on the present principal part, including the imperfect, participles, etc.

The following chart outlines the pattern for the combination of vowels in the conjugation of contract verbs.

αω

α + ε → α	α + ει → ᾳ	α + ο → ω
α + η → α	α + η → ᾳ	α + ου → ω
		α + ω → ω

εω

ε + ε → ει	ε + η → η	ε + ο → ου
ε + ει → ει	ε + η → η	ε + ου → ου
		ε + ω → ω

οω

ο + ε → ου	ο + η → ω	ο + ει → οι
ο + ο → ου	ο + ω → ω	ο + ῃ → οι
ο + ου → ου		

The uncontracted form of the verb is never found in written New Testament Greek.

b. The rule for accentuation of contracted verb forms is as follows: if either of the two contracting vowels received the accent in the *uncontracted* form, the accent will stay on the contracted syllable.

$$ἀγαπάετε → ἀγαπᾶτε$$

If neither of the contracting vowels had the accent in the *uncontracted* form, the normal rules for verb accentuation are followed.

$$ἠγάπαον → ἠγάπων$$

Note the accentuation patterns on the paradigms below.

c. The only stem (principal part) where contraction takes place is in the present system. The other principal parts follow the normal rules. In forming the other principal parts, however, the contracting vowel lengthens to its corresponding long vowel (α and ε to η, ο to ω) before the addition of the suffixes or endings, e.g., ποιέω, ποιήσω, ἐποίησα, πεποίηκα, πεποίημαι, ἐποιήθην.

d. Here are some representative conjugations of the contract verbs in the present system.

αω

Present Active Indicative (and Subjunctive)

	Singular	Plural
1st person	ὁρῶ	ὁρῶμεν
2nd person	ὁρᾷς	ὁρᾶτε
3rd person	ὁρᾷ	ὁρῶσι(ν)

Infinitive   ὁρᾶν

εω

Imperfect Middle/Passive Indicative

1st person	ἐφιλούμην	ἐφιλούμεθα
2nd person	ἐφιλοῦ	ἐφιλεῖσθε
3rd person	ἐφιλεῖτο	ἐφιλοῦντο

οω

Present Active Indicative

1st person	πληρῶ	πληροῦμεν
2nd person	πληροῖς	πληροῦτε
3rd person	πληροῖ	πληροῦσι(ν)

Infinitive   πληροῦν

Note the patterns of accentuation.

Note also that the indicative and subjunctive forms of the -αω conjugation are identical. Context must determine which mood is intended.

Vocabulary

Verbs:

ἀγαπάω	love
ἀκολουθέω	follow (with dative)
ἐλευθερόω	free, set free
γεννάω	beget, be born
ζάω	live
καλέω	call, summon, invite
λαλέω	speak
μαρτυρέω	witness
μισέω	hate
περιπατέω	walk around, live
πληρόω	make full, fill
ποιέω	do, make
προσκυνέω	worship (with dative)

σταυρόω   crucify
τηρέω   keep
τιμάω   honor
φανερόω   make manifest
φιλέω   love

Exercises

A.   Translate into English:

1. ἀγαπῶμεν τὸν θεὸν ἵνα μαρτυρῶμεν τῷ τιμῶντι τὸν κακόν.

2. πᾶς ὁ περιπατῶν κατὰ πνεῦμα ἀγαπήσει τοὺς μισοῦντας τοὺς υἱοὺς τοῦ φωτός.

3. δεῖ ὑμᾶς γεννηθῆναι ἄνωθεν.

4. ἠγάπησεν γὰρ ὁ θεὸς τὸν κόσμον, ὥστε τὸν υἱὸν τὸν μονογενῆ ἔπεμψεν, ἵνα πᾶς ὁ πιστεύων εἰς αὐτὸν μὴ καταλύηται ἀλλ᾽ ἔχῃ ζωήν.

5. ἐὰν μή τις γεννηθῇ ἐξ ὕδατος καὶ πνεύματος, οὐ δύναται εἰσελθεῖν εἰς τὴν βασιλείαν τοῦ θεοῦ.

6. ταῦτα αὐτοῦ λαλοῦντος πολλοὶ ἐπίστευσαν εἰς αὐτόν. ἔλεγεν οὖν ὁ Ἰησοῦς πρὸς τοὺς πιστεύσαντας αὐτῷ· ἐὰν ὑμεῖς μένητε ἐν τῷ λόγῳ μου, μαθηταί μού ἐστε, καὶ γνώσεσθε τὴν ἀλήθειαν, καὶ ἡ ἀλήθεια ἐλευθερώσει ὑμᾶς.

B.   Translate into Greek:

1. This man will love and hate those things which witness to the ones who crucified the lord.

2. To be born of the spirit is to love according to the ones who hate sin.

3. They were witnessing to the people who were hating the world.

4. The good prophets are honoring the priests who worshiped the God of glory.

LESSON XXIII

1. The Imperative Mood

a. The imperative mood is used in Greek, as it is in English, to express wishes, commands, entreaties, pleas, etc. The usual translation of the imperative in English is a direct command: "(You) close the door," "(You) answer the question." The understood subject is "you" (singular or plural). In Greek, however, there is also a third person imperative analogous to the English jussive (and parallel to the Greek hortatory subjunctive), e.g., "Let them come into the house," "Let her begin to worship."

b. The imperative is found only in the present and aorist forms. The difference is *kind of action*.

c. The present imperative is formed by finding the present stem and adding the following endings:

Active

	Singular	Plural
2nd person	-ε	-ετε
3rd person	-ετω	-ετωσαν

λῦε	loose	λύετε	loose
λυέτω	let him, her, it loose	λυέτωσαν	let them loose

118

Middle/Passive

2nd person	-ου	-εσθε
3rd person	-εσθω	-εσθωσαν

λύου	loose yourself; be loosed	λύεσθε	loose yourselves; be loosed
λυέσθω	let him, her, it loose (one) self; let him, her, it be loosed	λυέσθωσαν	let them loose themselves; let them be loosed

d. The first aorist imperative is formed by finding the first aorist stem (λυσ-) and adding the following endings:

Active

	Singular	Plural
2nd person	-ον	-ατε
3rd person	-ατω	-ατωσαν

λῦσον	loose	λύσατε	loose
λυσάτω	let him, her, it loose	λυσάτωσαν	let them loose

Middle

2nd person	-αι	-ασθε
3rd person	-ασθω	-ασθωσαν

λῦσαι	loose yourself	λύσασθε	loose yourselves
λυσάσθω	let him, her, it loose (one-)self	λυσάσθωσαν	let them loose themselves

e. The second aorist imperative is formed by finding the second aorist stem (e.g., βαλ-) and adding the same endings that were added to the present imperative.

Active

	Singular		Plural
βάλε	throw	βάλετε	throw
βαλέτω	let him, her, it throw	βαλέτωσαν	let them throw

Middle

	Singular		Plural
βαλοῦ	throw yourself	βάλεσθε	throw your-selves
βαλέσθω	let him-, her-, it-throw (one-)self	βαλέσθωσαν	let them throw themselves

Note the irregular accent on the second aorist middle singular second person of the imperative. Some few second aorist verbs are accented "irregularly" on the second person singular active, e.g., εἰπέ, ἐλθέ, εὑρέ.

f. The aorist passive imperative is formed by finding the aorist passive stem (λυθ-) and adding the following endings:

	Singular	Plural
2st person	-ητι	-ητε
3rd person	-ητω	-ητωσαν

λύθητι	be loosed	λύθητε	be loosed
λυθήτω	let him, her, it be loosed	λυθήτωσαν	let them be loosed

g. *The Present Imperative of* εἰμί

	Singular		Plural
2nd person	ἴσθι be	ἔστε	be
3rd person	ἔστω let him, her, it be	ἔστωσαν	let them be

2. Prohibition

The Greek language has several ways to express prohibition.

a. The present tense of the imperative is used with μή to indicate that one should stop an action already in process.

μὴ κρίνετε Do not judge (*better:* Stop judging).

b. The aorist *subjunctive* is used with μή to indicate that one should not begin a certain course of action.

μή λύσητε Do not loose (*better:* Do not
begin to loose).

c. The use of μή with the aorist imperative is a simple negative command or wish.

μὴ φιλήσατε τὸν κόσμον Do not love the world.

Vocabulary

Verbs:

βασανίζω	torment
σπλαγχνίζομαι	have compassion
φονεύω	kill, murder
ψεύδομαι	lie (tell a falsehood)

Nouns:

ἡ αὐλή	court
τὸ ἔθος, τοῦ ἔθους	custom
ἡ ἐλευθερία	freedom
ὁ οἰκοδεσπότης	householder
τὸ ὅραμα, τοῦ ὁράματος	vision
ἡ σπουδή	haste, diligence

Negative Particle:

οὐδέ	and not

Exercises

A. Translate into English:

1. ὁ ἔχων τὴν ἀγάπην τοῦ θεοῦ ἀκουέτω.

2. πορεύθητι εἰς τὴν βασιλείαν εἰς τὸ ἔρχεσθαι εἰς ζωήν.

3. τὸ τέλος ἐρχέσθω τοῦ τὸν λῃστὴν κρίνεσθαι ὑπὸ τοῦ πλήθους τῆς δικαιοσύνης.

4. εἰπὲ ταῦτα τῷ οἴκῳ τοῦ Ἰσραὴλ ἵνα τὰ ὁράματα τοῦ προφήτου κηρυχθῇ ἐν σπουδῇ.

5. μὴ φονεύετε τοὺς υἱοὺς τῆς αὐλῆς ὅτι πάντες ἐλεύσονται εἰς κρίσιν.

6. καὶ αὕτη ἐστὶν ἡ μαρτυρία τοῦ Ἰωάννου, ὅτε οἱ ἱερεῖς ἤρχοντο πρὸς αὐτὸν ἵνα ἀκολουθήσωσιν αὐτῷ.

7. ἐγεννήθησαν οὐδὲ ἐκ θελήματος σαρκὸς οὐδὲ ἐκ θελήματος ἀνδρὸς ἀλλ' ἐκ θεοῦ.

8. μὴ βάλε λίθους ὅτι οἱ υἱοὶ τῆς βασιλείας πεπίστευκαν.

B. Translate into Greek:

1. Stop leading the children of light into the place of darkness.

2. Do not begin to eat the bread of the householder.

3. Do not hate the things of the kingdom in order that you may enter into life.

Lesson XXIV

1. Future and Aorist of Liquid Stem Verbs

a. Some verbs end with a consonant called a liquid. These are λ, ν, ρ (and sometimes μ). Such consonants reject the sigma, which causes some deviations from the usual patterns for the future and aorist conjugations.

b. Since the sign of the future is ordinarily a σ added to the verb stem, and since the liquid consonants reject the σ, an epsilon (ε) is added to liquid stem verbs to compensate for the loss of the sigma. It has already been noted that the Greek language does not tolerate a line of vowels coming together, and thus such vowels coalesce or contract. The same holds true for the future of liquid stem verbs.

The stem of the verb is found (κρίνω→κριν-). Because ν- rejects the sigma, ε is added instead (κρινε-). Then one adds the usual endings for the future: κρινέω, etc. It can be seen immediately that the future of a liquid stem verb will be formed in the same manner as the present tense of a contract verb of the εω type (see Lesson XXII 1 a).

Future Active

	Singular	Plural
1st person	κρινῶ	κρινοῦμεν
2nd person	κρινεῖς	κρινεῖτε
3rd person	κρινεῖ	κρινοῦσι(ν)

Future Middle

1st person	κρινοῦμαι	κρινούμεθα
2nd person	κρινῇ	κρινεῖσθε
3rd person	κρινεῖται	κρινοῦνται

c. The first aorist of the liquid stem verb also must vary since the -σ- suffix is one of the characteristics of this form. In the aorist, however, the rejection of the sigma is compensated for by lengthening the primary vowel of the verb stem. The pattern is as follows: α→η; ε→ει; ι→ῑ; υ→ῡ (one will recall that there are no long marks written in Greek, so the long iota and upsilon must be "understood"). One then adds the usual first aorist endings to the verb. For example, the verb μένω:

	Singular	Plural
1st person	ἔμεινα	ἐμείναμεν
2nd person	ἔμεινας	ἐμείνατε
3rd person	ἔμεινε(ν)	ἔμειναν

Infinitive   μεῖναι

Note that not all liquid stem verbs have a liquid aorist; some have other forms for the aorist. In general a lexicon should be consulted for each verb.

2. Perfect Participle

a. The perfect active participle is built on the perfect stem and is declined as follows:

Singular

	Masculine	Feminine	Neuter
Nom.	λελυκώς	λελυκυῖα	λελυκός
Gen.	λελυκότος	λελυκυίας	λελυκότος
Dat.	λελυκότι	λελυκυίᾳ	λελυκότι
Acc.	λελυκότα	λελυκυῖαν	λελυκός

Plural

Nom.	λελυκότες	λελυκυῖαι	λελυκότα
Gen.	λελυκότων	λελυκυιῶν	λελυκότων
Dat.	λελυκόσι(ν)	λελυκυίαις	λελυκόσι(ν)
Acc.	λελυκότας	λελυκυίας	λελυκότα

b. The perfect middle/passive participle is built on the perfect middle/passive principal part. The middle/passive ending -μενος, -η, -ον is added directly to the perfect middle/passive stem, giving λελυμένος, -η, -ον. This is declined exactly like ἀγαθός, except for the accent.

Note that the accent falls on the penult throughout.

c. The translation of the perfect participle is essentially the same as for the aorist. The difference lies in the underlying *kind of action* — undefined for the aorist, perfective for the perfect.

3. Reflexive Pronouns

Reflexive pronouns are found only in the oblique cases and are combinations of αὐτός and the personal pronouns: ἐμαυτοῦ, of myself; σεαυτοῦ, of yourself; ἑαυτοῦ, of himself (herself, itself).

First Person - ſ

	Masculine	**Feminine**
Gen.	ἐμαυτοῦ	ἐμαυτῆς
Dat.	ἐμαυτῷ	ἐμαυτῇ
Acc.	ἐμαυτόν	ἐμαυτήν

Second Person - ſ

	Masculine	**Feminine**
Gen.	σεαυτοῦ	σεαυτῆς
Dat.	σεαυτῷ	σεαυτῇ
Acc.	σεαυτόν	σεαυτήν

Third Person - ſ

	Masculine	Feminine	Neuter
Gen.	ἑαυτοῦ	ἑαυτῆς	ἑαυτοῦ
Dat.	ἑαυτῷ	ἑαυτῇ	ἑαυτῷ
Acc.	ἑαυτόν	ἑαυτήν	ἑαυτόχ

Plural

	Masculine	Feminine	Neuter
Gen.	ἑαυτῶν	ἑαυτῶν	ἑαυτῶν
Dat.	ἑαυτοῖς	ἑαυταῖς	ἑαυτοῖς
Acc.	ἑαυτούς	ἑαυτάς	ἑαυτά

Note that the plural is the same for all three persons. The correct translation must be determined from the context, usually determined by the subject of the sentence or clause.

Vocabulary

Verbs:

ἀποθανοῦμαι	deponent future of ἀποθνήσκω
ἀποκτείνω	kill
ἐκτείνω	stretch out
κρίνω	judge

Exercises

A. Translate into English:

1. δεῖ ὑμῖν ἀποκτεῖναι τοὺς κακοὺς ἵνα μείνωμεν σὺν τοῖς υἱοῖς τοῦ φωτός.

2. ἀπ' ἐμαυτοῦ οὐκ ἐλήλυθα, ἀλλὰ πᾶς ὁ λελυκὼς τὸ πνεῦμα τοῦ φωτὸς κρινεῖ τὸν κόσμον τοῦ σκότους.

3. ἀπέστειλα αὐτοὺς εἰς τὸν κόσμον ἵνα πάντες ἀποστείλωσιν ἀγαθὰ δῶρα τῷ πεπιστευκότι ἐν τῷ ὀνόματι τοῦ Ἰησοῦ.

4. ἀποθανούμεθα ἐν ταῖς ἁμαρτίαις ἡμῶν ἐὰν μὴ ἀποστείλωμεν τοὺς ἱερεῖς ἑαυτῶν εἰς τὴν κώμην αὐτῶν.

5. πᾶς ὁ γεγεννημένος ἐκ τοῦ θεοῦ ἁμαρτίαν οὐ ποιεῖ, ὅτι σπέρμα δικαιοσύνης ἐν αὐτῷ μενεῖ.

6. μὴ θαυμάζετε, ἀδελφοί, εἰ μισεῖ ὑμᾶς ὁ κόσμος.

7. καὶ πᾶς ὁ ἀγαπῶν τὸν υἱὸν ἀγαπᾷ τὸν γεγεννημένον ἐξ αὐτοῦ.

8. αὕτη ἐστὶν ἡ μαρτυρία τοῦ θεοῦ ὅτι μεμαρτύρηκεν περὶ τοῦ υἱοῦ αὐτοῦ, τοῦ ἄγοντος πάντας εἰς τὴν ἀλήθειαν.

B. Translate into Greek:

1. The one who has been born of God has borne witness to the word of life.

2. I am not able to act of myself but by the power of God.

3. Our children have gone to the ones who have entered into evil.

LESSON XXV

1. Comparatives and Superlatives of Adjectives

a. In English the adjective has three "degrees" or "states": the positive (or usual form, e.g., good, sweet), the comparative (better, sweeter), and the superlative (best, sweetest). The Greek adjective also has these three degrees or states, and, generally speaking, the usages agree with English usage. In New Testament Greek, however, the superlative degree is rarely found; the comparative does double duty for both the comparative and superlative. The context determines which is appropriate. When the superlative is found, it usually indicates a degree of elation translated by "very" or "exceedingly."

b. The usual way of forming the comparative degree of the adjective is to add the suffix -τερ- to the stem of the adjective and decline it as a first and second declension adjective: -τερος, -α, -ον. The connecting vowel is either ο or ω, e.g., σόφος, σοφώτερος, -α, -ον.

c. The usual way of forming the superlative degree of the adjective is to add the suffix -τατ- to the stem of the adjective and decline it as a first and second declension adjective: -τατος, -η, -ον. The connecting vowel is either ο or ω, e.g., σόφος, σοφώτατος, -η, -ον.

d. When forming the comparative or superlative of a third declension adjective, the same procedure is followed but the connecting vowel is ε, e.g., ἀληθής, ἀληθέτερος (comparative), ἀληθέτατος (superlative).

e. Some adjectives form the comparison by ending in -ων or -ιων and are declined like μείζων (the comparative of μέγας).

128

Singular

	Masc. and Fem.	Neuter
Nom.	μείζων	μεῖζον
Gen.	μείζονος	μείζονος
Dat.	μείζονι	μείζονι
Acc.	μείζονα‑α μεῖζω	μεῖζον

Plural

	Masc. and Fem.	Neuter
Nom.	μείζονες	μείζονα‑α μεῖζω
Gen.	μειζόνων	μειζόνων
Dat.	μείζοσι(ν)	μείζοσι(ν)
Acc.	μείζονας	μείζονα‑α μεῖζω

f. Comparatives and superlatives have a recessive accent.

g. There are, of course, some irregular adjectives. Some of the more important ones are the following:

Positive	*Comparative*	*Superlative*
ἀγαθός	κρείσσων	κράτιστος
κακός	χείρων	
	ἥσσων	
μικρός	ἐλάσσων	ἐλάχιστος
πολύς	πλείων	πλεῖστος
	πλέων	

h. There are three ways to express comparison in Greek.

   i. By using the comparative degree of the adjective followed by a noun or pronoun in the genitive case:

   ἔρχεται δὲ ὁ ἰσχυρότερός μου.
   (Literally, "There is coming one stronger from me.")
   There comes one stronger than I.

ii. By using an adjective in the comparative degree with ἤ (than):

ἐκείνοις ἔσται κρεῖσσων ἤ ταύταις ὅτε ὁ υἱὸς ἔρχεται.
It will be better for those men than for these women when the son comes.

In these instances the case of the nouns to be compared will be the same.

iii. μᾶλλον connected with ἤ is generally used to compare nouns, phrases, or sometimes clauses. No comparative degree of the adjective is needed (since μᾶλλον is already comparative). If an adjective is present, it will be in the positive degree.

καὶ ἠγάπησαν οἱ ἄνθρωποι μᾶλλον τὸ σκότος ἤ τὸ φῶς.
And men loved the darkness more than the light.

2. Adverbs

a. Most adverbs (mechanically speaking) are formed from the adjective by substituting -ς for -ν on the genitive plural form (masculine or neuter): καλός, good; καλῶς, well.

b. The comparative degree of the adverb is the neuter singular accusative of the comparative of the adjective: σοφώτερον, more wisely.

c. The superlative degree of the adverb is the neuter plural accusative of the superlative of the adjective: σοφώτατα, most wisely.

d. There are some irregular adverbs too! Here are the most common.

Positive	*Comparative*	*Superlative*
εὖ (well)	βέλτιον	
κακῶς	ἧσσον	
-----	μᾶλλον (more)	μάλιστα
πολύ	πλεῖον	
	πλέον	

Vocabulary

Verbs:

αἰτέω	ask for
ἐρωτάω	ask a question
ζητέω	seek
θεάομαι	behold, see
λυπέω	grieve
νικάω	conquer, be victorious
ὁράω	see
παρακαλέω	beseech, exhort, encourage
τελειόω	end, complete
τυφλόω	blind, make blind
φοβέομαι	fear, be afraid
φωνέω	call

Exercises

A. Translate into English:

1. Ἰησοῦς ποιεῖ πλείονας μαθητὰς ἢ Ἰωάννης.
2. ὁ βασιλεύς ἐστιν μείζων τῶν φοβουμένων τὸν κακόν.
3. νενίκηκα τοὺς ζητοῦντας ἀποκτείνειν με.
4. μὴ λύπει ὅτι τὸ ἀσθενὲς τοῦ θεοῦ ἰσχυρότερον τῶν ἀνθρώπων.
5. μακάριόν ἐστιν μᾶλλον λαμβάνειν τὴν βασιλείαν τοῦ θεοῦ ἢ πέμπειν τὰ τέκνα τοῦ σκότους εἰς τὸν οἶκον τοῦ κακοῦ.

6. μείζονα ταύτης ἀγάπην πολλοὶ οὐκ ἔχουσιν.
7. ὁ κακὸς ἔμεινεν ἐν τοῖς κρείσσοσι τόποις ἵνα οἱ ἀγαθοὶ πέσωσιν εἰς τὴν βασιλείαν τῆς ἁμαρτίας;

B. Translate into Greek:

1. The world rejoices for the one greater than men.
2. It is exceedingly good to bear fruit in the kingdom of God.
3. Greater wisdom will lead the ones hearing the truth into the paths of righteousness.

Lesson XXVI

1. Conjugation of -μι Verbs

a. There are two primary conjugations in Greek: the -ω (omega) conjugation, which has been introduced up to this point, and the -μι conjugation. In the -ω verbs, the present principal part ends in -ω (or -ομαι if deponent). A verb whose present principal part ends in -μι is a -μι verb. These verbs were almost replaced completely by the ω conjugation by the *koinē* period, but a few of these verbs still were used.

Each of these verbs is different, and the peculiarities of each must be learned. There are several guidelines to assist in identifying the appropriate forms of the -μι verbs.

   i. The -μι verbs are different from the -ω verbs in only the present and aorist active principal parts. In the future, perfect, perfect middle/passive, and aorist passive these verbs have principal parts that follow the -ω patterns.

   ii. The present and aorist systems may be easily distinguished, because the present forms *reduplicate* and the aorist forms do not. The present tenses of the -μι verbs reduplicate with -ι- rather than an -ε- (as in the perfect); e.g., δο-, root meaning "give"; διδο- = reduplicated form. The -μι ending is added and the -ο- lengthens to -ω-, resulting in the verb δίδωμι, give.

   iii. Since no -μι verb is used in all of its forms in New Testament Greek, several representative

133

conjugations will be given for illustrative purposes. If the above guidelines are kept in mind, there will be little difficulty in recognizing the appropriate forms of the -μι verbs.

iv. There are four primary -μι verbs found in the New Testament: δίδωμι, ἵστημι, τίθημι, and a few forms of ἵημι (these are also found in combination with prepositions, just as the basic verb roots).

2. Conjugation of δίδωμι

The principal parts of the verb δίδωμι are the following: δίδωμι, δώσω, ἔδωκα, δέδωκα, δέδομαι, ἐδόθην.

a. *The Present System*

Present Active Indicative

	Singular	Plural
1st person	δίδωμι	δίδομεν
2nd person	δίδως	δίδοτε
3rd person	δίδωσι(ν)	διδόασι(ν)

Present Active Subjunctive

	Singular	Plural
1st person	διδῶ	διδῶμεν
2nd person	διδῷς	διδῶτε
3rd person	διδῷ	διδῶσι(ν)

Present Active Imperative

2nd person	δίδου	δίδοτε
3rd person	διδότω	διδότωσαν

Present Active Infinitive

διδόναι

Present Active Participle

Singular

	Masculine	Feminine	Neuter
Nom.	διδούς	διδοῦσα	διδόν
Gen.	διδόντος	διδούσης	διδόντος
Dat.	διδόντι	διδούσῃ	διδόντι
Acc.	διδόντα	διδοῦσαν	διδόν

The plural is declined exactly like the normal present active participle except for the accent.

Imperfect Active Indicative

	Singular	Plural
1st person	ἐδίδουν	ἐδίδομεν
2nd person	ἐδίδους	ἐδίδοτε
3rd person	ἐδίδου	ἐδίδοσαν

Note again that the distinguishing mark of the present stem of this verb (and most -μι verbs) is the reduplication with the iota, διδ-. The other forms of this verb (built on the present stem) can be easily recognized when they occur.

b. *The Aorist System*

The aorist active indicative of δίδωμι is conjugated exactly like the first aorist except for the fact that this aorist has -κ- instead of -σ- as its distinguishing mark, i.e., ἔδωκα, ἔδωκας, ἔδωκε, etc.

Aorist Active Subjunctive

	Singular	Plural
1st person	δῶ	δῶμεν
2nd person	δῷς	δῶτε
3rd person	δῷ	δῶσι(ν)

Aorist Active Imperative

2nd person	δός	δότε
3rd person	δότω	δότωσαν

Aorist Active Infinitive

δοῦναι

Aorist Active Participle

δούς δοῦσα δόν

The aorist active participle of this verb (and, again, most -μι verbs) is identical in endings to the present active participle. The only difference is that the present has the reduplication with iota.

3. Conjugation of ἴστημι

The principal parts of the verb ἴστημι are the following: ἴστημι, στήσω, ἔστησα (ἔστην), ἔστηκα, ἔσταμαι, ἐστάθην.

a. *The Present System*

Present Active Indicative

	Singular	Plural
1st person	ἴστημι	ἴσταμεν
2nd person	ἴστης	ἴστατε
3rd person	ἴστησι(ν)	ἰστᾶσι(ν)

Present Active Infinitive

ἱστάναι

Present Active Participle

ἱστάς ἱστᾶσα ἱστάν

The present active participle of ἵστημι has the same endings added to the stem ἱστ- as the endings already learned for πᾶς.

    b. The aorist active of ἵστημι — ἔστην — is conjugated with the same endings as ἐλύθην. ἔστησα, another aorist form, is formed exactly like the regular aorist indicative. The difference between ἔστησα and ἔστην is that the former is transitive (set, placed) and the latter is intransitive (stood).

    Aorist Infinitive: στῆναι

    Aorist Participle: στάς, στᾶσα, στάν (compare the present active participle of ἵστημι above).

    c. The other forms can be recognized easily.

Vocabulary

Verbs:

ἀγοράζω	buy
ἀνίστημι	raise up, rise
ἀποδίδωμι	give back, give up; restore, pay; sell (in middle)
δίδωμι	give
ἵστημι	stand, place, cause to stand
καθίστημι	set down, appoint
παραδίδωμι	deliver over, betray
παρίστημι	place beside, stand by

Conjunction:

οὖν	then, therefore (postpositive)

Interrogative:

πόθεν	whence? from where?

Exercises

A. Translate into English:

1. παντὶ αἰτοῦντί σε δίδου.

2. ὑμῖν δέδοται γινώσκειν τὰ μυστήρια τῆς βασιλείας τοῦ θεοῦ.

3. δῶμεν ἢ μὴ δῶμεν τὰ δῶρα τοῦ θεοῦ παντί;

4. πόθεν ἀγοράσωμεν ἄρτους ἵνα φάγωσιν οὗτοι;

5. καὶ ἀναστὰς ὁ δοὺς τὸ καλὸν δῶρον εἰσῆλθεν εἰς τὴν αὐλήν.

6. ἐσθιόντων δὲ αὐτῶν λαβὼν ὁ Ἰησοῦς ἄρτον καὶ δοὺς τοῖς μαθηταῖς εἶπεν· λάβετε, φάγετε, τοῦτό ἐστιν τὸ σῶμά μου.

7. οἱ οὖν ἄνθρωποι ἰδόντες ὅτι Ἰησοῦς ἐποίησεν σημεῖον ἔλεγον ὅτι οὗτός ἐστιν ἀληθῶς ὁ προφήτης ὁ ἐρχόμενος εἰς τὸν κόσμον.

8. γινώσκομεν ὅτι πάντες ἀναστήσονται ἐν τῇ ἀναστάσει ἐν τῇ ἐσχάτῃ ἡμέρᾳ.

B.   Translate into Greek:

1. The kings of the people were willing to stand before the throne of the king of kings.

2. He has given many things to those standing beside the priests.

3. The Son of Man will rise in order that the good things of this world may be restored in the temple of God.

LESSON XXVII

1. Conjugation of τίθημι

The principal parts of the verb τίθημι are the following: τίθημι, θήσω, ἔθηκα, τέθεικα, τέθειμαι, ἐτέθην.

a. *The Present System*

Present Active Indicative

	Singular	Plural
1st person	τίθημι	τίθεμεν
2nd person	τίθης	τίθετε
3rd person	τίθησι(ν)	τιθέασι(ν)

Present Active Subjunctive

	Singular	Plural
1st person	τιθῶ	τιθῶμεν
2nd person	τιθῇς	τιθῆτε
3rd person	τιθῇ	τιθῶσι(ν)

Present Active Imperative

2nd person	τίθει	τίθετε
3rd person	τιθέτω	τιθέτωσαν

Present Active Infinitive: τιθέναι

Present Active Participle: τιθείς, τιθεῖσα, τιθέν

The endings on the present active participle of τίθημι are identical to the endings used in the aorist passive participle.

b. *The Aorist System*

Aorist Active Imperative

2nd person	θές	θέτε
3rd person	θέτω	θέτωσαν

Aorist Active Infinitive: θεῖναι

Aorist Active Participle: θείς, θεῖσα, θέν

Compare the present active participle of τίθημι above.

2. Characteristics of ἀφίημι

The verb ἀφίημι is a compound of ἀπό and ἵημι. Only a few forms of ἵημι occur in the New Testament, usually in the compound ἀφίημι. The present tense forms have -ι- in the conjugation, and the aorist -ε- (or no vowel visible).

ἀφίετε = present
ἄφετε = aorist

3. Aorist of γινώσκω and βαίνω

Several verbs in the New Testament follow the -ω conjugation with the exception of the aorist active principal part, which follows the older -μι aorist form. Two of the more widely used are γινώσκω and βαίνω. The translation is, of course, not affected by the difference in form, e.g., "I knew," "I went," respectively.

a. The aorist of the verb γινώσκω is as follows

	Singular	**Plural**
1st person	ἔγνων	ἔγνωμεν
2nd person	ἔγνως	ἔγνωτε
3rd person	ἔγνω	ἔγνωσαν

Infinitive   γνῶναι

b. The conjugation of the aorist of the verb βαίνω is as follows. Note the aorist passive endings.

	Singular	**Plural**
1st person	ἔβην	ἔβημεν
2nd person	ἔβης	ἔβητε
3rd person	ἔβη	ἔβησαν

Infinitive   βῆναι

4. Conjugation of οἶδα

οἶδα is an old perfect used as a present, meaning "know."

Present *(perfect)*

	Singular	**Plural**
1st person	οἶδα	οἴδαμεν
2nd person	οἶδας	οἴδατε
3rd person	οἶδε(ν)	οἴδασι(ν)

Imperfect (old pluperfect)

	Singular	**Plural**
1st person	ᾔδειν	ᾔδειμεν
2nd person	ᾔδεις	ᾔδειτε
3rd person	ᾔδει	ᾔδεισαν

Infinitive: εἰδέναι

Participle: εἰδώς, εἰδυῖα, εἰδός

This participle is declined according to the normal perfect active participle form.

Vocabulary

Verbs:

ἀφίημι	permit, leave, forgive
ἐπιτίθημι	lay upon
μετανοέω	repent
παρατίθημι	set before, commit
προστίθημι	add, give in addition
τίθημι	place, put

Exercises

A.   Translate into English

1. εἰς τὰς χεῖράς σου παρατίθεμαι τὸ πνεῦμά μου.

2. ποῦ ἔθηκαν τὸ σῶμα τοῦ κυρίου ἡμῶν;

3. καὶ ἀναστάς τις εἶπεν ὅτι οἱ ἄνδρες ποιοῦσιν πολλὰ τοῖς μετανοοῦσιν τῶν ἁμαρτιῶν.

4. αὐτῶν ἐπιθέντων τὰς χεῖρας αὐτοῖς ὁ ἱερεὺς ἄρχεται δοῦναι τοῖς τέκνοις τὸν ἄρτον φαγεῖν.

5. δίδαξον ἡμᾶς προσεύχεσθαι ἵνα μείνωμεν ἐν τῷ οἴκῳ τοῦ θεοῦ.

6. οἴδαμεν δὲ ὅτι ὁ υἱὸς τοῦ θεοῦ ἤγγικεν, καὶ δέδωκεν ἡμῖν καινὴν διαθήκην ἵνα γινώσκωμεν τὸν ἀληθινόν.

7. μείζονα τούτων ὄψῃ. καὶ λέγει αὐτῷ· ἀμὴν, ἀμὴν λέγω ὑμῖν ὄψεσθε τὸν οὐρανὸν καὶ τοὺς ἀγγέλους τοῦ θεοῦ ἀναβαίνοντας καὶ καταβαίνοντας ἐπὶ τὸν υἱὸν τοῦ ἀνθρώπου.

8. μετὰ τοῦτο κατέβη εἰς τὴν πόλιν καὶ ἔμειναν οὐ πολλὰς ἡμέρας.

B. Translate into Greek

1. Having gone down into the water, Jesus was baptized by the prophet.

2. Did the disciples wish to know concerning the laying on of hands?

3. We knew that many evil children were giving gifts to the priests of the kingdom of sin.

LESSON XXVIII

1. The Optative Mood

a. There is yet another mood in Greek, the optative. By the *koinē* or New Testament period, however, most of the functions of this mood had been taken over by the subjunctive. Both the subjunctive mood and the optative mood designate doubt, hesitancy, or contingency, but the optative carries the nuance of extreme doubt, hesitancy, or contingency. Since it is difficult usually to draw a line between doubt and extreme doubt, it is easy to see why the optative came to be little used.

b. There are basically two usages of the optative found in the New Testament

  i. The optative may express a wish or hope, e.g., "May God fill you with joy" (cf. Romans 15:13). Sometimes the wish can be made very strongly: the expression μὴ γένοιτο is used by Paul quite frequently and is usually translated "God forbid!" "Certainly not!" "Never!" It literally means "Let it not happen." The optative can also be used as an analogous parallel to the cohortative subjunctive (cf. Philemon v. 20).

  ii. The fourth class conditional sentence uses the optative mood. This sentence is like the third class conditional in that the condition is unfulfilled, but here there is only a remote possibility of its being fulfilled. The pattern for this construction (no *whole* example of which is found in the New Testament) is this:

144

The remainder of the cardinals are indeclinable. The ordinals are declined as first and second declension adjectives.

4. Declension of οὐδείς

This word, a combination of the negative particle οὐ and the numeral "one" means "no one," "nothing."

Masculine	Feminine	Neuter
οὐδείς	οὐδεμία	οὐδέν
οὐδενός	οὐδεμιᾶς	οὐδενός
οὐδενί	οὐδεμιᾷ	οὐδενί
οὐδένα	οὐδεμίαν	οὐδέν

Note that μηδείς, μηδεμία, μηδέν will be used with non-indicative moods.

Vocabulary

Verbs:

διψάω	thirst
δηλόω	make manifest, show
εὐχαριστέω	give thanks
θεωρέω	behold
πίνω	drink

Adverb:

ὅπου	where, ~~since~~
οὔπω	not yet

Exercises

A. Translate into English:

1. καὶ ὁ πιστεύων εἰς ἐμὲ οὐ μὴ διψήσει.

2. οὐ Μωϋσῆς ἔδωκεν ὑμῖν τὸν νόμον;

3. μένωμεν ἐν ἁμαρτίᾳ; μὴ γένοιτο.

4. ἐάν τις διψᾷ, ἐρχέσθω πρός με καὶ πινέτω.

5. ὁ πιστεύων ἐν τῷ ὀνόματι τοῦ χριστοῦ οὐ μὴ εἴπῃ κακὰ ὅτι αὐτὸς οὐ δουλεύει δυσὶ κυρίοις.

6. ἐμὲ οἴδατε καὶ οἴδατε πόθεν εἰμί. καὶ ἀπ᾽ ἐμαυτοῦ οὐκ ἐλήλυθα ἀλλ᾽ ἐστὶν ἀληθινὸς ὁ πέμψας με ὃν ὑμεῖς οὐκ οἴδατε. ἐγὼ οἶδα αὐτόν, ὅτι παρ᾽ αὐτοῦ εἰμι καί με ἀπέστειλεν.

7. μὴ γὰρ ἐκ τῆς Γαλιλαίας ὁ χριστὸς ἔρχεται; οὐχ ἡ γραφὴ εἶπεν ὅτι ἐκ τοῦ σπέρματος Δαυίδ, καὶ ἀπὸ Βηθλέεμ τῆς κώμης ὅπου ἦν Δαυίδ, ἔρχεται ὁ χριστός;

8. αὐτοῦ ἰδόντος τὴν βασιλείαν ἐλθεῖν πόλλοι ἐλάμβανον τὴν μαρτυρίαν τοῦ θεοῦ.

9. οὐκ εἰμὶ ὁ μαθητὴς τοῦ κυρίου;

10. ἐάν τις θέλῃ τὸ θέλημα αὐτοῦ ποιεῖν, γνώσεται περὶ τῆς διδαχῆς ταύτης.

B. Translate into Greek:

1. The one who follows the evil one will definitely be led into the houses of sin.

2. Is not this one the prophet of the lord? By no means!

TABLES AND CHARTS

The Definite Article

Singular			Plural		
Masc.	*Fem.*	*Neut.*	*Masc.*	*Fem.*	*Neut.*
ὁ	ἡ	τό	οἱ	αἱ	τά
τοῦ	τῆς	τοῦ	τῶν	τῶν	τῶν
τῷ	τῇ	τῷ	τοῖς	ταῖς	τοῖς
τόν	τήν	τό	τούς	τάς	τά

First Declension Nouns

	Singular	Plural
Nom.	γραφή	γραφαί
Gen.	γραφῆς	γραφῶν
Dat.	γραπῇ	γραφαῖς
Acc.	γραφήν	γραφάς
Voc.	γραφή	γραφαί
Nom.	Βασιλεία	βασιλεῖαι
Gen.	βασιλείας	βασιλειῶν
Dat.	βασιλείᾳ	βασιλείαις
Acc.	βασιλείαν	βασιλείας
Voc.	βασιλεία	βασιλεῖαι
Nom.	γλῶσσα	γλῶσσαι
Gen.	γλώσσης	γλωσσῶν
Dat.	γλώσσῃ	γλώσσαις
Acc.	γλῶσσαν	γλώσσας
Voc.	γλῶσσα	γλῶσσαι

149

Masculine Nouns of the First Declension

	Singular	*Plural*
Nom.	μαθητής	μαθηταί
Gen.	μαθητοῦ	μαθητῶν
Dat.	μαθητῇ	μαθηταῖς
Acc.	μαθητήν	μαθητάς
Voc.	μαθητής	μαθηταί

Second Declension Nouns
Masculine

	Singular	**Plural**
Nom.	ὄχλος	ὄχλοι
Gen.	ὄχλου	ὄχλων
Dat.	ὄχλῳ	ὄχλοις
Acc.	ὄχλον	ὄχλους

Neuter

Nom.	τέκνον	τέκνα
Gen.	τέκνου	τέκνων
Dat.	τέκνῳ	τέκνοις
Acc.	τέκνον	τέκνα

Third Declension Nouns

Nom.	σάρξ	σάρκες
Gen.	σαρκός	σαρκῶν
Dat.	σαρκί	σαρξί(ν)
Acc.	σάρκα	σάρκας

Nom.	χάρις	χάριτες
Gen.	χάριτος	χαρίτων
Dat.	χάριτι	χάρισι(ν)
Acc.	χάριν	χάριτας

Nom.	ῥῆμα	ῥήματα
Gen.	ῥήματος	ῥημάτων
Dat.	ῥήματι	ῥήμασι(ν)
Acc.	ῥῆμα	ῥήματα

Nom.	ἄφεσις	ἀφέσεις
Gen.	ἀφέσεως	ἀφέσεως
Dat.	ἀφέσει	ἀφέσεσι(ν)
Acc.	ἄφεσιν	ἀφέσεις

Nom.	γραμματεύς	γραμματεῖς
Gen.	γραμματέως	γραμματέων
Dat.	γραμματεῖ	γραμματεῦσι(ν)
Acc.	γραμματέα	γραμματεῖς

Nom.	γένος	γένη
Gen.	γένους	γενῶν
Dat.	γένει	γένεσι(ν)
Acc.	γένος	γένη

First and Second Declension Adjectives
Singular

	Masculine	*Feminine*	*Neuter*
Nom.	ἀγαπητός	ἀγαπητή	ἀγαπητόν
Gen.	ἀγαπητοῦ	ἀγαπητῆς	ἀγαπητοῦ
Dat.	ἀγαπητῷ	ἀγαπητῇ	ἀγαπητῷ
Acc.	ἀγαπητόν	ἀγαπητήν	ἀγαπητόν

Plural

Nom.	ἀγαπητοί	ἀγαπηταί	ἀγαπητά
Gen.	ἀγαπητῶν	ἀγαπητῶν	ἀγαπητῶν
Dat.	ἀγαπητοῖς	ἀγαπηταῖς	ἀγαπητοῖς
Acc.	ἀγαπητούς	ἀγαπητάς	ἀγαπητά

Third Declension Adjectives

	Singular		*Plural*	
	Masc./Fem.	*Neut*	*Masc./Fem.*	*Neut.*
Nom.	ἀσθενής	ἀσθενές	ἀσθενεῖς	ἀσθενῆ
Gen.	ἀσθενοῦς	ἀσθενοῦς	ἀσθενῶν	ἀσθενῶν
Dat.	ἀσθενεῖ	ἀσθενεῖ	ἀσθενέσι(ν)	ἀσθενέσι(ν)
Acc.	ἀσθενῆ	ἀσθενές	ἀσθενεῖς	ἀσθενῆ

Declension of μείζων

Nom.	μείζων	μεῖζον	μείζονες (μείζους)	μείζονα (ω)
Gen.	μείζονος	μείζονος	μειζόνων	μειζόνων
Dat.	μείζονι	μείζονι	μείζοσι(ν)	μείζοσι(ν)
Acc.	μείζονα (μείζω)	μεῖζον	μείζονας (ους)	μείζονα (ω)

Declension of πᾶς

Singular

	Masc.	*Fem.*	*Neut.*
Nom.	πᾶς	πᾶσα	πᾶν
Gen.	παντός	πάσης	παντός
Dat.	παντί	πάσῃ	παντί
Acc.	πάντα	πᾶσαν	πᾶν

Plural

Nom.	πάντες	πᾶσαι	πάντα
Gen.	πάντων	πασῶν	πάντων
Dat.	πᾶσι(ν)	πάσαις	πᾶσι(ν)
Acc.	πάντας	πάσας	πάντα

Present Participle of εἰμί

Singular

	Masc.	*Fem.*	*Neut.*
Nom.	ὤν	οὖσα	ὄν
Gen.	ὄντος	οὔσης	ὄντος
Dat.	ὄντι	οὔσῃ	ὄντι
Acc.	ὄντα	οὖσαν	ὄν

Plural

Nom.	ὄντες	οὖσαι	ὄντα
Gen.	ὄντων	οὐσῶν	ὄντων
Dat.	οὖσι(ν)	οὔσαις	οὖσι(ν)
Acc.	ὄντας	οὔσας	ὄντα

Present Active Participle

Singular

Nom.	λύων	λύουσα	λῦον
Gen.	λύοντος	λυούσης	λύοντος
Dat.	λύοντι	λυούσῃ	λύοντι
Acc.	λύοντα	λύουσαν	λῦον

Plural

Nom.	λύοντες	λύουσαι	λύοντα
Gen.	λυόντων	λυουσῶν	λυόντων
Dat.	λύουσι(ν)	λυούσαις	λύουσι(ν)
Acc.	λύοντας	λυούσας	λύοντα

First Aorist Active Participle
Singular

Nom.	λύσας	λύσασα	λῦσαν
Gen.	λύσαντος	λυσάσης	λύσαντος
Dat.	λύσαντι	λυσάσῃ	λύσαντι
Acc.	λύσαντα	λύσασαν	λῦσαν

Plural

Nom.	λύσαντες	λύσασαι	λύσαντα
Gen.	λυσάντων	λυσασῶν	λυσάντων
Dat.	λύσασι(ν)	λυσάσαις	λύσασι(ν)
Acc.	λύσαντας	λυσάσας	λύσαντα

Second Aorist Active Participle
Singular

Nom.	ἐλθών	ἐλθοῦσα	ἐλθόν
Gen.	ἐλθόντος	ἐλθούσης	ἐλθόντος
Dat.	ἐλθόντι	ἐλθούσῃ	ἐλθόντι
Acc.	ἐλθόντα	ἐλθοῦσαν	ἐλθόν

Plural

Nom.	ἐλθόντες	ἐλθοῦσαι	ἐλθόντα
Gen.	ἐλθόντων	ἐλθουσῶν	ἐλθόντων
Dat.	ἐλθοῦσι(ν)	ἐλθούσαις	ἐλθοῦσι(ν)
Acc.	ἐλθόντας	ἐλθούσας	ἐλθόντα

Perfect Active Participle
Singular

Nom.	λελυκώς	λελυκυῖα	λελυκός
Gen.	λελυκότος	λελυκυίας	λελυκότος
Dat.	λελυκότι	λελυκυίᾳ	λελυκότι
Acc.	λελυκότα	λελυκυῖαν	λελυκός

Plural

Nom.	λελυκότες	λελυκυῖαι	λελυκότα
Gen.	λελυκότων	λελυκυιῶν	λελυκότων
Dat.	λελυκόσι(ν)	λελυκυίαις	λελυκόσι(ν)
Acc.	λελυκότας	λελυκυίας	λελυκότα

Present Middle/Passive Participle
Singular

Nom.	λυόμενος	λυομένη	λυόμενον
Gen.	λυομένου	λυομένης	λυομένου
Dat.	λυομένῳ	λυομένῃ	λυομένῳ
Acc.	λυόμενον	λυομένην	λυόμενον

Plural

Nom.	λυόμενοι	λυόμεναι	λυόμενα
Gen.	λυομένων	λυομένων	λυομένων
Dat.	λυομένοις	λυομέναις	λυομένοις
Acc.	λυομένους	λυομένας	λυόμενα

Perfect Middle/Passive Participle
Singular

Nom.	λελυμένος	λελυμένη	λελυμένον
Gen.	λελυμένου	λελυμένης	λελυμένου
Dat.	λελυμένῳ	λελυμένῃ	λελυμένῳ
Acc.	λελυμένον	λελυμένην	λελυμένον

Plural

Nom.	λελυμένοι	λελυμέναι	λελυμένα
Gen.	λελυμένων	λελυμένων	λελυμένων
Dat.	λελυμένοις	λελυμέναις	λελυμένοις
Acc.	λελυμένους	λελυμένας	λελυμένα

First Aorist Middle Participle
Singular

Nom.	λυσάμενος	λυσαμένη	λυσάμενον
Gen.	λυσαμένου	λυσαμένης	λυσαμένου
Dat.	λυσαμένῳ	λυσαμένῃ	λυσαμένῳ
Acc.	λυσάμενον	λυσαμένην	λυσάμενον

Plural

Nom.	λυσάμενοι	λυσάμεναι	λυσάμενα
Gen.	λυσαμένων	λυσαμένων	λυσαμένων
Dat.	λυσαμένοις	λυσαμέναις	λυσαμένοις
Acc.	λυσαμένους	λυσαμένας	λυσάμενα

Second Aorist Middle Participle
Singular

Nom.	ἐλθόμενος	ἐλθομένη	ἐλθόμενον
Gen.	ἐλθομένου	ἐλθομένης	ἐλθομένου
Dat.	ἐλθομένῳ	ἐλθομένῃ	ἐλθομένῳ
Acc.	ἐλθόμενον	ἐλθομένην	ἐλθόμενον

Plural

Nom.	ἐλθόμενοι	ἐλθόμεναι	ἐλθόμενα
Gen.	ἐλθομένων	ἐλθομένων	ἐλθομένων
Dat.	ἐλθομένοις	ἐλθομέναις	ἐλθομένοις
Acc.	ἐλθομένους	ἐλθομένας	ἐλθόμενα

First Aorist Passive Participle
Singular

Nom.	λυθείς	λυθεῖσα	λυθέν
Gen.	λυθέντος	λυθείσης	λυθέντος
Dat.	λυθέντι	λυθείσῃ	λυθέντι
Acc.	λυθέντα	λυθεῖσαν	λυθέν

Plural

Nom.	λυθέντες	λυθεῖσαι	λυθέντα
Gen.	λυθέντων	λυθεισῶν	λυθέντων
Dat.	λυθεῖσι(ν)	λυθείσαις	λυθεῖσι(ν)
Acc.	λυθέντας	λυθείσας	λυθέντα

Second Aorist Passive Participle
Singular

Nom.	γραφείς	γραφεῖσα	γραφέν
Gen.	γραφέντος	γραφείσης	γραφέντος
Dat.	γραφέντι	γραφείσῃ	γραφέντι
Acc.	γραφέντα	γραφεῖσαν	γραφέν

Plural

Nom.	γραφέντες	γραφεῖσαι	γραφέντα
Gen.	γραφέντων	γραφεισῶν	γραφέντων
Dat.	γραφεῖσι(ν)	γραφείσαις	γραφεῖσι(ν)
Acc.	γραφέντας	γραφείσας	γραφέντα

Contract Verbs

αω

Present Active

Ind.	Subj.	Impv.	Inf.
τιμῶ	τιμῶ		
τιμᾷς	τιμᾷς	τιμᾶ	
τιμᾷ	τιμᾷ	τιμάτω	
τιμῶμεν	τιμῶμεν		τιμᾶν
τιμᾶτε	τιμᾶτε	τιμᾶτε	
τιμῶσι(ν)	τιμῶσι(ν)	τιμάτωσαν	

Present Middle/Passive

τιμῶμαι	τιμῶμαι		
τιμᾷ	τιμᾷ	τιμῶ	
τιμᾶται	τιμᾶται	τιμάσθω	
τιμώμεθα	τιμώμεθα		τιμᾶσθαι
τιμᾶσθε	τιμᾶσθε	τιμᾶσθε	
τιμῶνται	τιμῶνται	τιμάσθωσαν	

Imperfect Active

ἐτίμων
ἐτίμας
ἐτίμα
ἐτιμῶμεν
ἐτιμᾶτε
ἐτίμων

Imperfect Middle/Passive

ἐτιμώμην
ἐτιμῶ
ἐτιμᾶτο
ἐτιμώμεθα
ἐτιμᾶσθε
ἐτιμῶντο

εω

Present Active

Ind.	Subj.	Impv.	Inf.
φιλῶ	φιλῶ		
φιλεῖς	φιλῇς	φίλει	
φιλεῖ	φιλῇ	φιλείτω	
φιλοῦμεν	φιλῶμεν		φιλεῖν
φιλεῖτε	φιλῆτε	φιλεῖτε	
φιλοῦσι(ν)	φιλῶσι(ν)	φιλείτωσαν	

Present Middle/Passive

φιλοῦμαι	φιλῶμαι		
φιλῇ	φιλῇ	φιλοῦ	
φιλεῖται	φιλῆται	φιλείσθω	
φιλούμεθα	φιλώμεθα		φιλεῖσθαι
φιλεῖσθε	φιλῆσθε	φιλεῖσθε	
φιλοῦνται	φιλῶνται	φιλείσθωσαν	

Imperfect Active

ἐφίλουν
ἐφίλεις
ἐφίλει
ἐφιλοῦμεν
ἐφιλεῖτε
ἐφίλουν

Imperfect Middle/Passive

ἐφιλούμην
ἐφιλοῦ
ἐφιλεῖτο
ἐφιλούμεθα
ἐφιλεῖσθε
ἐφιλοῦντο

οω

Present Active

Ind.	Subj.	Impv.	Inf.
πληρῶ	πληρῶ		
πληροῖς	πληροῖς	πλήρου	
πληροῖ	πληροῖ	πληρούτω	
πληροῦμεν	πληρῶμεν		πληροῦν
πληροῦτε	πληρῶτε	πληροῦτε	
πληροῦσι(ν)	πληρῶσι(ν)	πληρούτωσαν	

Present Middle/Passive

πληροῦμαι	πληρῶμαι	
πληροῖ	πληροῖ	
πληροῦται	πληρῶται	
πληρούμεθα	πληρώμεθα	πληροῦσθαι
πληροῦσθε	πληρῶσθε	
πληροῦνται	πληρῶνται	

Imperfect Active

ἐπλήρουν
ἐπλήρους
ἐπλήρου
ἐπληροῦμεν
ἐπληροῦτε
ἐπλήρουν

Imperfect Middle/Passive

ἐπληρούμην
ἐπληροῦ
ἐπληροῦτο
ἐπληρούμεθα
ἐπληροῦσθε
ἐπληροῦντο

Principal Parts of
Some Irregular Verbs

Pres.	Fut.	Aor.	Perf.	Perf. M/P	Aor. Pass.
ἄγω	ἄξω	ἤγαγον	ἦχα	ἦγμαι	ἤχθην
αἴρω	ἀρῶ	ἦρα	ἦρκα	ἦρμαι	ἤρθην
*ἀνοίγω	ἀνοίξω	ἤνοιξα	ἀνέῳγα	ἀνέῳγμαι	ἠνεῴθην
ἀποθνῄσκω	ἀποθανοῦμαι	ἀπέθανον	τέθνηκα		
ἀποστέλλω	ἀποστελῶ	ἀπέστειλα	ἀπέσταλκα	ἀπέσταλμαι	ἀπεστάλην
ἀφίημι	ἀφήσω	ἀφῆκα	ἀφεῖκα	ἀφεῖμαι	ἀφείθην
βαίνω	βήσομαι	ἔβην	βέβηκα		
γίνομαι	γενήσομαι	ἐγενόμην	γέγονα	γεγένημαι	ἐγενήθην
γινώσκω	γνώσομαι	ἔγνων	ἔγνωκα	ἔγνωσμαι	ἐγνώσθην
δίδωμι	δώσω	ἔδωκα	δέδωκα	δέδομαι	ἐδόθην
δύναμαι	δυνήσομαι				ἠδυνήθην or ἐ
ἔρχομαι	ἐλεύσομαι	ἦλθον	ἐλήλυθα		
ἐσθίω	φάγομαι	ἔφαγον			
ἔχω	ἕξω	ἔσχον	ἔσχηκα		
λαμβάνω	λήμφομαι	ἔλαβον	εἴληφα	εἴλημμαι	ἐλήμφθην
λέγω	ἐρῶ	εἶπον	εἴρηκα	εἴρημαι	ἐρρέθην
ξηραίνω		ἐξήρανα		ἐξήραμμαι	ἐξηράνθην
ὁράω	ὄψομαι	εἶδον	ἑώρακα	ὦμμαι (ἑώραμαι)	ὤφθην
πάσχω	πείσομαι	ἔπαθον	πέπονθα		
πίνω	πίομαι	ἔπιον	πέπωκα	πέπομαι	ἐπόθην
τίθημι	θήσω	ἔθηκα	τέθεικα	τέθειμαι	ἐτέθην
φέρω	οἴσω	ἤνεγκα	ἐνήνοχα	ἐνήνεγμαι	ἠνέχθην
χαίρω	χαρήσομαι				ἐχάρην

*For other forms of ἀνοίγω, consult your lexicon.

Greek-English Vocabulary

ἀγαθός, -η, -ον good
ἀγαπάω love
ἡ ἀγάπη love
ἀγαπητός, -η, -ον beloved
ὁ ἄγγελος messenger, angel
ἁγιάζω sanctify, consecrate
ἅγιος, -α, -ον holy
ἀγοράζω buy, purchase
ὁ ἀγρός field
ἄγω go, lead, bring
ὁ ἀδελφός brother
τὸ αἷμα, αἵματος blood
αἴρω take up, take away
αἰτέω ask, ask for
ὁ αἰών, αἰῶνος age
αἰώνος, -ον eternal
ἀκολουθέω follow (with dative)
ἀκούω hear, obey (with genitive or accusative)
ἡ ἀλήθεια truth
ἀληθής, ἀληθές true
ἀληθινός true
ἀλλά but (strong adversative)
ἀλλότριος, -α, -ον strange, belonging to another
ἁμαρτάνω sin, miss the mark
ἡ ἁμαρτία sin, missing the mark
ὁ ἀμπελών, ἀμπελῶνος vineyard

ἄν particle, not translatable but signifies modality
ἀνά up, upwards (with accusative)
ἀναβαίνω go up
ἀναγινώσκω read
ἡ ἀνάστασις, ἀναστάσεως resurrection
ὁ ἀνήρ, ἀνδρός man, husband
ὁ ἄνθρωπος man, mankind (humankind)
ἀνίστημι cause to rise, raise; stand up, arise (middle)
ἀνοίγω open
ὁ ἄνεμος wind
ἡ ἀνομία lawlessness
ἀντί instead of (with genitive)
ἄνωθεν from above, again
ἄξιος, -α, -ον worthy, comparable, corresponding
ἀπαγγέλλω announce, declare
ἀπό from (with genitive)
ἀποδίδωμι give back, pay; sell (middle)
ἀποθνῄσκω die
ἀποκτείνω kill
ἀπολύω release, dismiss
ἀποστέλλω send out
ὁ ἀπόστολος apostle, one sent out

160

ἀρά   therefore
ὁ ἄρτος   bread, loaf
ἡ ἀρχή   beginning
ὁ ἀρχιερεύς, ἀρχιερέως   chief
   priest
ἄρχω   rule (with genitive);
   begin (middle)
ὁ ἄρχων, ἄρχοντος   ruler,
   prince
ἡ ἀσθένεια   weakness,
   sickness
ἀσθενής, ἀσθενές   sick, weak
ἀσπάζομαι   salute, greet
ἡ αὐλή   court
αὐτός, -η, -ο   same; himself,
   etc.; he, she, it, they
ἡ ἄφεσις, ἀφέσεως   forgiveness
ἀφίημι   forgive, allow, let go,
   leave

βαίνω   go (only in com-
   pounds in the NT)
βάλλω   throw, cast
βαπτίζω   baptize
τὸ βάπτισμα   baptism
βασανίζω   torture, torment
ἡ βασιλεία   kingdom
ὁ βασιλεύς, βασιλέως   king
βασιλεύω   rule, reign
βαστάζω   take up, carry, bear
τὸ βιβλίον   book, scroll
βλέπω   see
τὸ βρῶμα, βρώματος   food

γάρ   for (postpositive)
γεννάω   beget, be born
τὸ γένος, γένους   race
γίνομαι   become, come into
   being, happen

γινώσκω   know
γνωρίζω   make known, reveal
ἡ γνῶσις, γνώσεως   knowledge
ὁ γονεύς, γονέως   parent
τὸ γράμμα, γράμματος   letter
ὁ γραμματεύς, γραμματέως
   scribe
ἡ γραφή   writing
γράφω   write
ἡ γυνή, γυναικός   woman, wife

τὸ δαιμόνιον   demon
δέ   but, and (postpositive)
δεῖ   it is necessary
δεξιός, -α, -ον   right (opposed
   to left)
δέχομαι   receive
δηλόω   make manifest, show
διά   through (with genitive);
   because of, on account of
   (with accusative)
ἡ διαθήκη   covenant
ἡ διακονία   service, ministry
ὁ διδάσκαλος   teacher
διδάσκω   teach
δίδωμι   give
δίκαιος, -α, -ον   righteous
ἡ δικαιοσύνη   righteousness
διψάω   thirst
διώκω   pursue, persecute
ἡ δόξα   glory
δοξάζω   glorify
δουλεύω   be a slave, serve;
   obey (with dative)
ὁ δοῦλος   slave
δύναμαι   be able
ἡ δύναμις, δυνάμεως   power
τὸ δῶρον   gift

ἐάν   if (with subjunctive)
ἐγγίζω   draw near
ἐγγύς   near
ἐγείρω   raise
τὸ ἔθνος, ἔθνους   nation,
   Gentile
τὸ ἔθος, ἔθους   custom
εἰ   if
εἰμί   to be
ἡ εἰρήνη   peace
εἰς   into (with accusative)
εἰσέρχομαι   go in, enter
ἐκ   out of (with genitive)
ἕκαστος, -η, -ον   each
ἐκβάλλω   throw out, cast out
ἐκεῖ   there
ἐκεῖνος, -η, -ο   that
   (demonstrative pronoun)
ἐκλεκτός, -η, -ον   chosen,
   elect
ἐκτείνω   stretch out
τὸ ἔλεος, ἐλέους   mercy, compassion, pity
ἐλπίζω   hope
ἡ ἐλπίς, ἐλπίδος   hope
ἡ ἐλευθερία   freedom
ἐλευθερόω   set free, free
ἔμπροσθεν   before, in the
   presence of
ἐν   in (with dative)
ἡ ἐξουσία   power, authority
ἡ ἑορτή   feast
ἡ ἐπαγγελία   promise
ἐπί   upon, on, at, on top of
   (with dative)
ἐπιγινώσκω   come to know,
   recognize
ἐπιστρέφω   turn, return
ἐπιτίθημι   lay upon

τὸ ἔργον   work
ἡ ἔρημος   desert, wilderness
ἔρχομαι   come, go
ἐρωτάω   ask
ἐσθίω   eat
ἔσχατος, -η, -ον   last
ἕτερος, -α, -ον   another,
   other, different
ἑτοιμάζω   prepare
ἕτοιμος, -η, -ον   prepared,
   ready
τὸ ἔτος, ἔτους   year
εὐαγγελίζομαι   preach the
   gospel
τὸ εὐαγγέλιον   good news,
   gospel
εὐθέως   immediately
εὐλογέω   bless
ἡ εὐλογία   blessing
εὑρίσκω   find
εὐχαριστέω   give thanks
ἔχω   have, hold

ζάω   live
ζητέω   seek
ἡ ζωή   life

ἤ   than, or
ἤδη   already
ἡ ἡμέρα   day
ἡμέτερος, -α, -ον   our

ὁ θάνατος   death
θαυμάζω   marvel, wonder
θεάομαι   behold
τὸ θέλημα, θελήματος   will
θέλω   wish, will
ὁ θερισμός   harvest

13

ὁ θεός God

θεραπεύω heal

—θεωρέω look at, observe

ἡ θλῖψις, θλίψεως tribulation

ὁ θρόνος throne

ἡ θυγάτηρ, θυγατρός daughter

ἡ θύρα door

ἡ θυσία sacrifice

θύω sacrifice

ἴδιος, -α, -ον one's own

ὁ ἱερεύς, ἱερέως priest

τὸ ἱερόν temple

Ἰησοῦς Jesus

ἱκανός, -η, -ον sufficient, able

τὸ ἱμάτιον garment

ἵνα in order that (with subjunctive)

ἵστημι stand, cause to stand

14

ἰσχυρός, -α, -ον strong

καθαρός, -α, -ον pure

καθαρίζω cleanse, purify

καθώς just as

καί and, even, also

ὁ καιρός (appointed) time

κακός, -η, -ον evil

καλέω call, summon

καλός, -η, -ον beautiful, good

ἡ καρδία heart

ὁ καρπός fruit

κατά down, down from (with genitive); according to, during (with accusative)

καταβαίνω go down

καταλύω destroy

κατεσθίω devour, tear to pieces

ἡ κεφαλή head

STOP for
test One

15

κηρύσσω proclaim, preach, announce

ὁ κληρονόμος heir

κοινός, -η, -ον common, unclean

ὁ κόσμος world

κράζω cry out

κρίνω judge

ἡ κρίσις, κρίσεως judgment

ἡ κτίσις, κτίσεως creation

ὁ κύριος lord, master

ἡ κώμη village

λαλέω speak

λαμβάνω take, receive

ὁ λαός people

λέγω say, speak

λείπω leave

16

ὁ λῃστής robber, thief

ὁ λίθος stone

ὁ λόγος word, saying, reason

λοιπός, -η, -ον rest, remaining

λυπέω grieve

λύω loose

ἡ μαρτυρία witness, testimony

ὁ μαθητής disciple, learner

μακάριος, -α, -ον happy, blessed

μᾶλλον more

μαρτυρέω bear witness

μέγας, μεγάλη, μέγαν large, great

μέλλω to be about to (do something)

μένω remain, abide

τὸ μέρος, μέρους part

μετά   with (with genitive);
  after (with accusative)
μετανοέω   repent
ἡ μετάνοια   repentance
μή   not (used with
  non-indicative)
μηδέ   and not, nor, not even
μηκέτι   no longer
μήποτε   lest perchance
ἡ μήτηρ, μητρός   mother
μικρός, -α, -ον   small
μισέω   hate
ὁ μισθός   wages, pay
τὸ μνημεῖον   tomb
μοιχεύω   commit adultery
μόνος, -η, -ον   only, alone
τὸ μυστήριον   mystery
μωρός, -α, -ον   foolish

ὁ ναός   temple
νεκρός, -α, -ον   dead
νικάω   conquer, be victorious
νομίζω   think, suppose
ὁ νόμος   law
νῦν   now
ἡ νύξ, νυκτός   night

ξένος, -η, -ον   strange
ξηραίνω   dry, dry up

ἡ ὁδός   way, path, road
οἶδα   know (old perfect form)
ἡ οἰκία   house
ὁ οἰκοδεσπότης   master of the
  house, steward
ὁ οἶκος   house
ὀλίγος, -η, -ον   few
ὅλος, -η, -ον   whole (in
  predicative position only)

τὸ ὄνομα, ὀνόματος   name
ὅπου   where (of place)
ὁράω   see
τὸ ὅραμα, ὁράματος   vision
ἡ ὀργή   wrath
τὸ ὄρος, ὄρους   mountain
ὅταν   whenever (with
  subjunctive)
ὅτε   when
ὅτι   that, because
οὐ (οὐκ, οὐχ)   not
οὐδέ   and not, not even, nor
οὐκέτι   no longer
οὖν   then, therefore
οὔπω   not yet
ὁ οὐρανός   heaven
οὔτε   and not
οὗτος, αὕτη, τοῦτο   this
  (demonstrative pronoun)
οὕτως   thus, in this manner
ὁ ὀφθαλμός   eye
ὁ ὄχλος   crowd

τὸ παιδίον   little child
πάλιν   again
παρά   from alongside (with
  genitive); in the presence
  of, at the side of (with
  dative); alongside (with
  accusative)
παραδίδωμι   deliver over,
  hand over
ἡ παράδοσις, παραδόσεως   tradition, that which is handed
  over or down
παρακαλέω   beseech, exhort
πᾶς, πᾶσα, πᾶν   every, all
πάσχω   suffer
ὁ πατήρ, πατρός   father

πείθω persuade

πειράζω test, put to the test

πέμπω send

περί concerning, about (with genitive); around (with accusative)

περιπατέω walk around, live

περισσός, -η, -ον abundant, excessive

πίνω drink

πίπτω fall

πιστεύω believe

ἡ πίστις, πίστεως faith

πιστός, -η, -ον faithful

τὸ πλῆθος, πλήθους multitude

πληρόω make full, fulfill

τὸ πλοῖον boat

τὸ πνεῦμα, πνεύματος spirit, wind

πόθεν from where? whence?

ποιέω make

ἡ πόλις, πόλεως city

πολύς, πολλή, πολύ much, many

πονηρός, -α, -ον evil

πορεύομαι proceed, go

τὸ ποτήριον cup

ποῦ where?

ὁ πούς, ποδός foot

πρό before (with genitive)

πρός toward (with accusative)

ἡ προσευχή prayer

προσεύχομαι pray

προσκυνέω worship, prostrate oneself (with dative)

προσφέρω bring to, offer

ὁ προφήτης prophet

πρῶτος, -η, -ον first

πτωχός, -η, -ον poor

πῶς how?

τὸ ῥῆμα, ῥήματος word

ἡ ῥίζα root

τὸ σάββατον Sabbath

σαλεύω shake, agitate

ἡ σάρξ, σαρκός flesh

τὸ σημεῖον sign

σήμερον today

ὁ σῖτος wheat

σκανδαλίζω cause to stumble

ἡ σκοτία darkness

τὸ σκότος, σκότους darkness

ἡ σοφία wisdom

σοφός, -η, -ον clever, skillful, wise

τὸ σπέρμα, σπέρματος seed

σπλαγχνίζομαι be moved with compassion

ἡ σπουδή diligence

σταυρόω crucify

στηρίζω establish, support

σύν with (with dative)

συνάγω gather together

ἡ συναγωγή assembly, synagogue

ἡ συνείδησις, συνειδήσεως conscience

σύρω drag, draw

ἡ σφραγίς, σφραγῖδος seal

σώζω save

τὸ σῶμα, σώματος body

ἡ σωτηρία salvation

τὸ τέκνον child

τὸ τέλος, τέλους end, conclusion, goal

τελειόω complete, finish

25 τηρέω   keep
τίθημι   put, place, lay
τιμάω   honor
τίς, τί   who? which? what?
τὶς, τὶ   someone, something anyone, anything
ὁ τόπος   place
ὁ τυφλός   blind man
τυφλόω   blind, make blind

τὸ ὕδωρ, ὕδατος   water
ὁ υἱός   son
ὑμέτερος, -α, -ον   your
26 ὑπάγω   go away, depart
ὑπακούω   obey (with genitive)
ὑπάρχω   exist, be
ὑπέρ   in behalf of (with genitive); beyond, more than (with accusative)
ὑπό   by (with genitive); under (with accusative)
ἡ ὑπομονή   steadfast endurance

φανερόω   manifest, make manifest
φέρω   bear, carry, bring
φημί   say
φιλέω   love
φίλος, -η, -ον   beloved, dear, loving; ὁ φίλος, friend

27 φοβέομαι   fear, be afraid
φονεύω   murder, kill
ἡ φυλακή   guard, prison, watch
φωνέω   call, summon
ἡ φωνή   voice, sound
τὸ φῶς, φωτός   light

χαίρω   rejoice
ἡ χαρά   joy
ἡ χάρις, χάριτος   grace
τὸ χάρισμα, χαρίσματος   free gift
ἡ χείρ, χειρός   hand
χορτάζω   eat to the full, be satisfied
ὁ χριστός   messiah, the anointed one
χρονίζω   spend time, tarry
ἡ χώρα   country
χωρίς   apart from, without (with genitive)

ψεύδομαι   lie, tell a falsehood
ἡ ψυχή   life, life-principle

ὧδε   here
ἡ ὥρα   hour
ὡς   as
ὥστε   so that (with infinitive of result)

BIBLIOGRAPHY

There are numerous books which can be useful to those who have completed their study of the basic elements of New Testament Greek. A good intermediate grammar is essential to examine further some of the more subtle nuances of Greek grammar and syntax. A good lexicon is also a "must."

Intermediate Grammars

Chamberlain, William D. *An Exegetical Grammar of the Greek New Testament*. New York: Macmillan, 1941.

Dana, H. E., and Julius R. Mantey. *A Manual Grammar of the Greek New Testament*. New York: Macmillan, 1927.

Hewett, James A. *New Testament Greek: A Beginning and Intermediate Grammar*. Peabody, MA: Hendrickson, 1986.

Robertson, A. T., and W. H. Davis. *A New Short Grammar of the Greek New Testament*. New York: Harper & Bros., 1935.

Advanced Grammars

Blass, F. W., and A. Debrunner. *A Greek Grammar of the New Testament and Other Early Christian Literature*. Translated and revised by R. W. Funk. Chicago: University of Chicago Press, 1961.

Robertson, A. T. *A Grammar of the Greek New Testament in the Light of Historical Research*. 3rd ed. London: Hodder & Stoughton, 1919.

Lexicons

Bauer, Walter. *A Greek-English Lexicon of the New Testament and Other Early Christian Literature*. Translated and edited by F. W. Gingrich and W. F. Arndt. Second edition, revised and augmented by F. W. Gingrich and F. Danker. Chicago: University of Chicago Press, 1979.

Gingrich, F. W. *A Shorter Lexicon of the Greek New Testament.* Second edition, revised by F. Danker. Chicago: University of Chicago Press, 1983.

Other Useful Resources

MacDonald, William G. *Greek Enchiridion: A Concise Handbook of Grammar for Translation and Exegesis.* Peabody, MA: Hendrickson, 1986.

Metzger, Bruce M. *Lexical Aids for Students of New Testament Greek.* New edition published by the author. Princeton, NJ: Theological Book Agency, 1969.

———. *The Text of the New Testament: Its Transmission, Corruption, and Restoration.* Second Edition. New York: Oxford University Press, 1968.

Aland, Kurt, and Barbara Aland. *The Text of the New Testament.* Grand Rapids, MI: Eerdmans, 1987. Revised edition, 1989.